Socrates, Jesus and Freedom

Socrates, Jesus and Freedom

A Philosophical Reflection

JOAN ARNSTEEN

Proud Daughter Publishing

Alger, MI

Copyright © 2016 by Joan Arnsteen

All rights reserved. No part of this publication may be reproduced, distributed, or transmitted in any form or by any means, without prior written permission.

Proud Daughter Publishing
1460 Joy Street
Alger, Michigan 48610
www.prouddaughterllc.com

Socrates, Jesus and Freedom - 1st edition
Written by Joan Arnsteen
Socratesplace.com

Cover and book design by Marion J Chard

ISBN - 978-0692748961
Library of Congress PCN - 2016933557

Socrates, Jesus and Freedom is dedicated to the loving memory of my sister Kay, who passed on September 11, 2014, and the loving memory of my Mom, Sara, who passed on September 16, 2014. I love you both and am missing you. The completion of this book would not be possible without the assistance of James T. Neumann, heaven's emissary, who came to me to repair my broken heart with his love.

Acknowledgments

The author wishes to express her thanks to Marion Chard, editor and publisher from Proud Daughter Publishing, whose professional services brought Socrates, Jesus and Freedom to publication.

Contents

Under the Spell of Philosophy

How Philosophy Can Move us Closer to God   1

The Delphic Oracle: Socrates and Freedom   15

The Divine Oracle: Jesus and Freedom   57

"Know Thyself": Socratic Wisdom   81

The Inspiration for Inductive Methodology   89

The *Republic*: The Good City   105

The Spirit of Freedom is Upon the Earth   135

The Nature of the Philosopher and the Good City   145

Passing of Night's Scepter to Day's Crown   151

Genesis: Intimate with God   171

Exodus and Moses: Man of God   203

Socrates, Love and the Symposium   209

God's *Agape* Love   223

"The Lord is There"   229

INTRODUCTION

Under the Spell of Philosophy

I came under the spell of Socrates at an early age, following his example and awakening from the amanuensis that, according to Socrates, plagues us all. When I reflected upon the care of the soul and quickening of the spirit that are tenets of Socratic teaching, I became aware of the parallels of the teaching of Socrates and Jesus. Socrates taught that the highest purpose of the human being was to care for one's soul and to be a lover of wisdom and by doing so we give birth to intellectual children (ideas) which will become immortal. Jesus taught us to "walk by faith, not by sight" (2 Cor 5:7 The *New Inductive Study Bible*).[1] There are many similarities between Socrates and Jesus Christ, for example, both men never wrote anything down but had a profound effect on their followers. Their spiritual influence remains as powerful today as it was in the past as the confluence of ancient Greek philosophical thought and Judeo-Christian religion are studied and understood within a complex territory of new ideas. Socrates' love for his fellow citizens is evident in the care that he took to guide the ancient Athenians in open conversations that led to the truth. The treasure of our Lord's love for us belongs to each of us as individuals, and belongs to the past, present, and future for all human beings. Our education and training are mission-oriented, as God's vision directs us; we then follow in obedience and with love. The love of Christ refers to both the love of Jesus Christ for humanity and each individual and our love and worship for Christ. Like Jesus, Socrates taught his followers to care for their souls, and both men (one divine and one human) taught using inductive reasoning, the art of dialectic (question and answer), and ancient symbols to impart their knowledge and wisdom. Both the philosopher and the Son of God claimed divine inspiration — Socrates from his *daimonia*, and Jesus from the Holy Father — as they taught their followers to "know thyself" (*gnothi sauton*) for an insight into our spiritual selves. We can vividly see the martyrdom of both men through the eyes of their devoted disciples, and — with our inquisitive natures and hearts open to love — we become the heirs of their teaching. When we think about Socrates, we are within the secular realm, and when we worship Christ with love and reverence, we enter the sacred realm, but this is not to say that these two realms are separated by time and space — the sacred realm is embedded into the secular realm as a diamond embedded into a rock. Our human workshop is within the secular realm, where we learn how to use the gifts of God in preparation for obedient discipleship within that sphere. This book is a measure of my devotion to Socrates, who was unique in his philosophical wisdom, as he taught the ancient Athenians the art of living a good life, virtue, and caring for their souls. The humble inspiration for this book flows from the teaching of Jesus Christ, who taught his followers the same virtues, (albeit holy virtues), and — for Christ-believers — He comes into our hearts to transform us in His image, and sharpen our spiritual hearing and eyesight. When we examine the teaching similarities between Socrates and Jesus Christ, we learn through study and devotion — to open our minds and hearts to the *agape* love that God has for us. God's Word teaches us that He designed our minds for an understanding of the Spirit of Truth and our souls for eternal life and joy. Both Socrates and Jesus encouraged questions that are in the spirit of a child, as we do our best to seek the truth, these questions will bring us closer to God.

The Divine Oracle and the Delphic Oracle, Jesus and Socrates, teach us about being human in the best sense, that is, as a loving creature of God. Both the King and the Philosopher orientate us within the time and place that anchor us as humans who look to God for our lessons on goodness, although God is outside of time. Philosophy is but a shadow of the divine, but we see the shadow before we see the light. My goal with this book, *Socrates, Jesus and Freedom,* is to bridge the gap between the mundane and the sacred for our growth as God's emissaries on earth. I hope to accomplish this goal by demonstrating the similarities between Socrates and Jesus' teaching techniques by examining inductive methodology. An analysis of parts of the *Holy Bible* and

Plato's Republic will serve as our framework to conduct this investigation. As a writer, I also aspire to tell a good non-fiction story that will engage the reader and provide many important questions that will send us on a search for answers. In the brief introductory chapter 1, "How Philosophy can Move us Closer to God", I introduce the inductive blueprint for us to begin thinking about both Socrates and Jesus' teaching through induction and dialectic. We become aware of the historical significance of ancient Greek philosophical thought and Judeo-Christian religion, and how studying both philosophy and religion will lead us to the truth. In chapter 2, "The Delphic Oracle: Socrates and Freedom", I introduce the reader to Socrates, the ancient Greek philosopher who was born in Athens in 469 B.C. and put to death in 399 B.C. Socrates' life-long mission was to discover if there was someone wiser than he was, in the belief that he did not have any wisdom. Socrates believed that his role was one of a "gadfly" — stinging his listeners out of their intellectual complacency. We look at the historical setting of 6th century Athens, and the impact that the new democracy had on Athena's children. We examine Athens through the eyes and ideas of Socrates, as we learn to care for our souls and develop virtue as Socrates taught — when he said, "Knowledge is virtue." In chapter 3, "The Divine Oracle: Jesus and Freedom", I introduce the reader to the ministry of Jesus through the Four Gospels — Mathew, Mark, Luke and John — harmonious books that shed light on our understanding of the life and teaching of Jesus. We learn the miraculous story of Jesus' ministry, the gathering of His disciples, and His death and resurrection. Jesus makes use of arguments that have a rabbinical precedent with an assertion and a contrast of ideas as He teaches His followers in an inductive manner. We learn that Jesus did not leave us as orphans, but left the power of the Holy Spirit to teach and guide us. In chapter 4, " 'Know Thyself' Socratic Wisdom", I pick up the golden thread of knowledge in ancient Athens, and weave its meaning into modernity in order to assist our growth as rational, spiritual and free human beings. In chapter 5, "The Inspiration for Inductive Methodology", I examine inductive reasoning and the art of dialectic, two methodologies used by Jesus and Socrates to teach their knowledge and wisdom. We learn that Jesus and Socrates were not dogmatic teachers, but taught in an inquisitive and spiritual manner. Socrates, for example, practiced inductive reasoning when he questioned others in search of a reasoning process moving from particulars to universals. Inductive methodology can provide us with the tools to reason, study, think, teach, learn, obtain premises and conclusions, question, answer, persuade, and come to hold beliefs. In chapter 6, "The *Republic*: The Good City", we will learn more about the historical Socrates and his cognitive theory through the pen of his most famous pupil, Plato. In the *Republic,* Socrates — the main narrator — defines justice, the character of a just city-state, and the just man. Socrates taught justice (*dikaiosune)*, and his teaching anticipates Christian ethics, goodness, and morality. We learn that justice is one of the main themes of God's Holy Word. In chapter 7, "The Spirit of Freedom is Upon the Earth", I examine the concept of freedom (taught by Jesus and Socrates) and what freedom means to us as individuals. I argue that human beings desire to be free, and so we pursue those things that will bring us spiritual growth, beauty, comfort, joy, peace, pleasure, and happiness. Freedom is the natural state of the human being and is our most essential characteristic. In chapter 8, "The Nature of the Philosopher and the Good City", I summarize the philosophy of individual freedom. I show how we yearn to be a spiritual person and how being free will set the pattern for an aesthetic enjoyment of life, and a clearer — intuitive — understanding of what it means to be free. In chapter 9, "The Passing of Night's Scepter to Day's Crown", I teach how to study Plato's dialogues and the Bible inductively by reasoning from specific propositions to general propositions. Socrates used induction in his cross-examination where he would have his subject set aside his or her prejudices in order to gain a clearer understanding of a concept or the topic under discussion. For our biblical studies, inductive methodology means that we will interpret the scripture without bringing our own pre-judgments or preconceived views to the interpretation. Our interpretation of the Bible is from specific and consistent text: the scripture is the source, its books are harmonious, and the whole is inerrant. In chapter 10, "Genesis: Intimate with God", I apply the inductive methodology to the Biblical book of Genesis, in order to learn about our Lord God, who is infinite, all-powerful, and created material matter out of non-material nothing. We learn how the creation story is a key to our own happy lives; we know by failure our own weaknesses, and by our strengths, we voluntarily choose God. Genesis is the river of truth that runs throughout the Bible and flows into the Book of Revelation. In chapter 11, "Exodus and Moses, Man of God", I bring Moses into our book about Jesus and Socrates, because we can learn more about ourselves if we apply Moses' story to our own actions. In practicing our inductive methodology that we have learned from Socrates, we can interpret Exodus as a revelation to us of the Holiness of God. In chapter 12, "Socrates, Love and the *Symposium*", I write that the similarities between Socrates and Jesus are bound together with love: love toward our fellow men and women, and love toward our Creator. God is *agape* love; love fulfills every law of God. Socrates was born in a pre-Christian era, but his message was also one of love. I teach Socrates' story of love to the reader through the *Symposium* from the dialogues of Plato. Chapter 13, "God's *Agape* Love", summarizes what we have learned through inductive methodology where we find a logical framework to process symbols, signs, and concepts, and how this method strengthens our faculties for the perception of the archetypes that God has given us for knowledge of Him. The Socratic notion of virtue was an idea within the concept of love. When the New Testament was written, there were four primary Greek words to describe the concept of love: *eros, stergo, phileo,* and *agape*. The love that God has for us is called *agape*, and this holy love is available through Christ who reconciles us to God. Through God's *agape* love, all things are possible: we choose life, not death; we choose truth, not falsehood, and we choose love, not hate. In the summary chapter 14, "The Lord is There" we remind ourselves that we all have opinions, beliefs, faith, trust, and seek the truth, as we set high aspirations, hope, and expectations for our family and ourselves. We are committed to discerning God's truth and laws, and we will act on this truth. We apply the theory of induction in order to understand Socrates' teaching that "virtue is knowledge." We also apply the theory of induction to the Gospels that record the Good Word. Through our inductive practice, we keep in mind what makes up a spiritually good city. God guides us in our development of His Word and he protects our soul from evil for the edification of His Kingdom. We are the earthly hands for the building of the New Testament Church — a holy place of worship that we call the City of God. This book, *Socrates, Jesus and Freedom,* is humbly presented for my love of Jesus Christ, "Your words were found and I ate them, And your words became a joy and the delight of my heart; For I have been called by Your name, O Lord God of hosts" (Jer 15:16).

CHAPTER ONE

How Philosophy Can Move us Closer to God

"My heart overflows with a good theme; I address my verses to the King; My tongue is the pen of a ready writer" (Psalms 45:1). The love of Christ is a central theme of Christian belief and theology, and we practice a return of this divine love by taking possession of our own souls. We take the initiative through both secular and sacred ideas, where we uncover ourselves through the study of spiritual ideas found, for example, in ancient Greek philosophical thought and Judeo-Christian religion. The ancient Greek philosopher, Socrates, taught that the highest purpose of the human being was to care for one's soul and to be a lover of wisdom and by doing so we will gain happiness. With our inquisitive natures and our hearts open to love, we become the heirs of the teaching of both Socrates and Jesus. Although they lived more than four centuries apart, they taught us to care for our souls through developing virtue and the art of living a good life. Both men claimed divine inspiration: Socrates from his *daimonia* (his divine voice that advised him on actions not to take), and Jesus from the Word of the Holy Father. Both men — one human and one divine — taught using ancient symbols, inductive reasoning, and dialectic, (i.e. the art of question and answer) to assist us in opening our minds to the truth, and our hearts to the *agape* love — God's love — that is a miraculous force for good in our world. This author humbly asks you, the reader, to take this inspirational journey with me to learn more about both men as we open our hearts and souls for eternal life and joy.

Socrates was a Greek philosopher born in 469 B.C. and put to death by hemlock in 399 B.C. on the charges of impiety, and corrupting the youth of the city. His death gave the enlightened Greeks a permanent black mark in history. Socrates tells the men of the jury whom have sentenced him to death, "Now the hour to part has come. I go to die, you go to live. Which of us goes to the better lot is known to no one, except the god."[2] Jesus of Nazareth was born between 6 and 4 B.C. in Galilee, and crucified between 30 and 36 A.D. (Scholars have defended various dates for Jesus' birth and death.) "Therefore when Jesus had received the sour wine, He said, 'It is finished' " (From the Greek Tetelestai, also translated "It is accomplished") (John 19:30). Jesus' divine mission on earth was accomplished — and the holy prophecy fulfilled — with His death on the cross. We think about Socrates' courage and calmness as he took the cup of hemlock; we also pray as we reflect upon our Lord's passion during the crucifixion. Socrates' teaching was epoch-making philosophy for ancient Athenians as well as for us today; Jesus' teaching was revolutionary during his lifetime as it is currently for our salvation. The following reflection on both men, Socrates and Jesus, is a meditation upon what they both taught us about our humanity, our individualism, our soul, and how we can successfully draw upon their wisdom. Our goal is to open our hearts to the love that was demonstrated through the teaching of both men — one human and one divine. Both Socrates and Jesus drew their listeners into the truth, in order for us to gain knowledge and wisdom, by caring (first and foremost) for our souls. The philosopher would coach his subject to set aside his (or her) prejudices in order to gain a clearer understanding of a concept or the topic under discussion. Similarly, Jesus also teaches us through induction, i.e., He demonstrates to us all of the particulars in order that we may understand the general term or meaning of the spiritual concept. For example, Jesus taught us about God and God's love for us by enumerating His Holy attributes, such as: love, goodness, infinity, righteousness, omnipotence, omnipresence, and omniscience.[3] Reasoning from the particular cases to the general idea or concept is a practice found throughout the pages of Plato's *Republic* where we learn, for example, the values of goodness, virtue, honesty, decency, courage, fidelity to the city, comradeship, friendship, and family — all particular values that are aspects of a good person living happily within a good metropolis. The inductive thesis is also consistent with the teaching — and our understanding of the *Holy Bible* — where our interpretation is from specific and consistent text, and the Books are harmonious and the whole is inerrant. "Now to Him who is able to establish you according to my gospel and the preaching of Jesus Christ, according to the revelation of the mystery which has been kept secret for long ages past" (Rom 16:25). "Only God is wise" (Rom 16:27).

    In *The Republic*, Glaucon tells Socrates, "A just person...will be whipped, stretched on a rack, chained, blinded with fire, and, at the end, when he has suffered every kind of evil, he'll be impaled, and will realize then that one shouldn't want to be just but to be believed to be just".[4] The perfectly just person was Jesus Christ who calls for forgiveness for his persecutors from the cross, "Father, forgive them; for they do not know what they are doing" (Luke 23:34). Sinless, gentle, meek and righteous — the "Son of Man", was a charismatic teacher with extraordinary and divine abilities, and he used many methods and forms to teach (most notably parables, poetry, similes, metaphors, and counter questions, see e.g. Mark 3:1-4). The two pedagogical methods which concern us in understanding both The Republic and the Bible are induction (pointing out the particular attributes in order to understand the general concept), and dialectic (the art of investigating or discussing the truth through question and answer). When the chief priests and scribes and the elders came to Jesus and asked Him, "By what authority are You doing these things, or who gives You this authority to do these things?" Jesus said to them, "I will ask you one question, and you answer Me, and *then* I will tell you by what authority I do these things. Was the baptism of John from heaven, or from men? Answer me." They *began* reasoning among themselves, saying, "If we say, 'From heaven,' He will say, 'Then why did you not believe him?' But shall we say, 'From men?' " — they were afraid of the people, for everyone considered John to have been a real prophet. Answering Jesus, they said, "We do not know." And Jesus said to them, "Nor will I tell you by what authority I do these things" (Mark 11:28-33).

"Great is the Lord, and greatly to be praised, In the city of our God, His holy mountain. Beautiful in elevation, the joy of the whole earth, Is Mount Zion in the far north, The city of the great King. God, in her palaces, Has made Himself known as a stronghold" (Psalms 48:1-3). "Oh send out Your light and Your truth, let them lead me; let them bring me to Your holy hill And to Your dwelling places" (Psalms 43:3). As we travel to the sacred Hills of Judaea, we take up our staff for the long and worshipful journey to the Mountain of God. God teaches us how to worship Him through our social and spiritual language, and verbalization and social interaction with our fellow men and women. God teaches us horizontally, men to men and women, and vertically, God to men and women — where our natural human understanding may transcend to a spark of wisdom, and wherein we might prayerfully, be reconciled in some degree with the highest spiritual order of God's plan for us. We want to stand upon this Holy Mount and hear His Sacred Voice, which alone will give us joy and quicken our spirit. "It came about when Moses was coming down from Mount Sinai (and the two tablets of the testimony were in Moses' hand as he was coming down from the mountain), that Moses did not know that the skin of his face shone because of his speaking with Him" (Ex 34:29). God remains hidden behind His creation, but we have certainty of His presence through His power in the universe, and His visible light and goodness. We labor for an increased knowledge of the unfathomable God, whom lovingly placed His Holy Word in our hands. As we study to show ourselves approved for the Lord, we know that the path to God is open for all of us through our Lord. We also humbly acknowledge Socrates, whose teaching has formed our rational patterns for clear thinking and understanding. Philosophy is not antithetical to our faith, but strengthens our faith because through our rationality we understand the unity of worship that flows from Moses and the Prophets — who foreordained the birth and teaching of the Messiah.

God's promises taught in the Old Testament have come to fruition in the Son. Jesus taught, "The time is fulfilled, and the kingdom of God is at hand; repent and believe in the gospel" (Mark 1:15). And He said, "Do not think that I came to abolish the Law or the Prophets; I did not come to abolish but to fulfill" (Mat 5:17). These sacred reasoning powers touch the periphery of heaven, and our faith and worship will then carry us forward to embrace the spiritual world. Transfigured by God's *agape* love for us, we remain humble in our prayers as we, "give thanks to the Lord, for He is good, for His loving kindness is everlasting" (Psalms 107:1).

Now is the best time to be born, to break the day as we stand here reflecting upon our souls: streaming light and subsuming whatever brilliance we may absorb. Our feet are on the earth and our hearts are in heaven, where we desire the queenly royal purple robes and fleur-de-lis symbols of the saints. The universal universe is patiently waiting for us as we become familiar with our souls: to fly, climb, swim, run, and enjoy those monumental elements that magically — by our God — have breathed life into us. Nourished by this essential universe, we color our palette with the splendid beauty of the divine. The beautifully patterned soul is the pocket that holds our dreams and desires; dressed for our worship and holiness unto the Lord. This heavenliness enters into our dreams and in awakening, we thank *Adoni* for light and life and love. Only the pure in heart shall see the cliff of a thousand faces; and only the pure in spirit shall climb one of those steep sides. Lightning and deafening thunder dissuade us from such an adventure — desire and dedication persuade us to go onward and upward, to continue the quest to the end. We calculate precisely for those lucky numerical combinations that will open the door to heaven's restful space. In time we are born, live and die; out of time the aesthetic experience of life becomes immortal.

We are like the eager students of ancient Greece who tied fresh and fragrant rosemary leaves in their hair for study and remembrance. Our stage is set in modern history, the play is knowledge, the art of the play is philosophy, and we must go beyond the historical in order to understand ourselves, and transcend philosophy within God's Holy Word in order to become free. A new philosophy — along with a heart of love — can serve as a guide for us to find our way back to God. Our individual personalities are formative chronicles that we write with the philosophical finger, and the figure animating the hand is the body of freedom. What does it mean to be human, and what does it mean to be free? The ancient Greek custom was to teach through myths — Homeric events that were believed by the Athenians to have once happened. The ancient Greeks used divination to predict events, for example, the flight of birds or the form of the liver of a sacrificed animal. Socrates also taught truth through myth, (see, for example, the Allegory of the Cave, the Platonic Theory of Forms, and the Myth of Er) but he thought that this addiction to divination was folly. The ancient Greeks lived in an enchanted world where the cosmic orders were dominant and controlled and influenced the behaviors of men. Greek religion focused upon action where myth and ritual secured the goodwill of the gods, and the main objective was to secure advancement in this life. The forms of behavior that were offensive to the gods were *hubris* (presumptuousness) and *atasthalie* (pride); however, the Greek religion did not guide the Athenians in their conduct, so for this direction, they turned to philosophy.

Although Socrates lived in this ancient civilization with its addiction to numerous gods and auguries, he was not superstitious. Socrates, who followed the custom of his time, also taught using myth, but these myths contained a kernel of truth and enlightened others to understand their own natures and the higher nature of their souls. Socrates (like Christ) also taught using allegories, because he knew that we could grasp the profound and spiritual side of our nature through allegoric examples and stories. Socrates (like Christ) taught using dialectic, which used a pattern of argumentation to examine each issue from several sides, explored the interplay of ideas, and then evaluated the ideas by reason — leaving room for the mystery of the spirit. For example, Biblical metaphors — buried deep in ancient meanings — come alive through dialectic. Our exile from heaven and our absence from God are painful to our souls; and all of these methods — myths, allegories, metaphors, inductive reasoning, and dialectic — are useful in helping us, God's creatures, move back to our spiritual home. Socrates wanted to "sting us out of our forgetfulness", and Christ wanted to awaken us to the power of the Holy Spirit within us. We joyfully love God and Christ while we are living in our secular space; imagine the unbounded glories as our eternal love for God and Christ unfolds in our heavenly realm. "You shall love the Lord your God with all your heart and with all your soul and with all your might" (Dt 6:5).

The citizens of blossoming Athens excelled in philosophy, mathematics, sculpture, architecture, gymnasium, plays, drama, science, poetry, and the formation of the new democracy. Socrates' philosophical stance about divine power and the obedience that we owe to the gods were not Bible-based beliefs, but he expressed ideas that were more sublime than any philosopher or thinker since his time. For the inquisitive Greeks, the world has been here since eternity, and the gods have been here even prior to that. The gods were all knowing — understanding all of your thoughts, and even your private intentions. Socrates prayed to the gods to grant him what is good, because he felt that the gods would know better than himself what he needed. Socrates devoted himself to virtue and living a virtuous life; and he instructed the young men in this behavior. Virtue (*arête*) was the ability or skill in some particular respect, for example, courage, wisdom, moderation or the skill to be fully human. We can be unequal in virtue, therefore, virtue is something that varies, but our desire to be good is universal. Socrates taught that no one knowingly desires what is bad, therefore the differences in our conduct is a consequence of our knowledge or lack thereof. Knowing what is right automatically results in the desire to do it.[5] Socrates' charisma attracted the Athenian youth to his side and he never accepted financial reward for his teaching. As a citizen and a man, his character was just and he behaved with dignity and virtue in everything that he did (even on the day of his death!).

The ancient Hellenistic orthodoxy of a pantheon of gods, whose jealousies and powers of retribution, soon evolved due to the Hellenes distrust of the wisdom of the gods. An increase in knowledge by the ancient population displaced a lot of superstition with a belief in fate. For the followers of Socrates, Plato, and Aristotle, the logical mind, reasoning, and questioning natures were superior to the old myths and superstitions of the Attic community. As seekers of wisdom, we dip into the icy waters of antiquity and sounding in this stream, recollection refreshes us, where we coax the philosophers to share their knowledge. Nevertheless, we do not learn knowledge of infinity from the philosophers, for even the stream's arced ring must be banked of earth. The Platonic concept of the cosmos taught that the many instances of things are only what they are in relationship to the one Idea. The Platonic Ideas are authentic archetypes that echo the knowledge of ancient days. The Platonic Doctrine of Recollection states that we already know what we need to know; our knowledge comes back to mind when we recall the eternal realities learned during a previous existence of the soul.[6]

The philosopher's sweet scent is from wisdom's perfume; the Christian's fragrance emanates from that which is Holy God. To build a bridge from the mundane to the sacred is a difficult task, however, a worthy and necessary one — where Socrates is the tutor for our human virtuous nature, and Christ is our teacher and Master for our spiritual nature. One man is human and one is holy, which tells us where we place our highest esteem for our commission. The grace of God was on Christ, as he grew stronger and increased in wisdom. "The Child continued to grow and become strong, increasing in wisdom; and the grace of God was upon Him" (Luke 2:40). Christ's maturity was demonstrated in obedience to God — the same obedience that he taught to us. "Since you have in obedience to the truth purified your souls for a sincere love of the brethren, fervently love one another from the heart, for you have been born again not of seed which is perishable but imperishable, that is, through the living and enduring word of God" (1 Pt 1:22-23). A Christian will experience a spiritual life and move to a greater joy and fulfillment in Christ. God's wisdom is sacred. In the pre-Christian era,

Socrates taught wisdom, virtue, and goodness and to care for our souls, and he lived his life as a righteous and good citizen; he exemplified the virtues in himself that he taught to others. Although he denied having wisdom, we can truly say that he was a sagacious tutor who led others to the truth regarding their own souls. Socrates was a profound and masterful philosopher, and we study him for enlightenment — but we can serve only one Master. Our heart belongs to Jesus Christ; however, we also pay respect to the greatest philosopher, Socrates, who taught us how to think.

Unlike the omnipotence of the Christian God, the ancient Greeks imposed limitations on divine power. Socrates did not believe that the gods were the cause of evil (as many believed), but were providers of happiness and good will. Socrates taught that the material body was greedy for pleasure and for the satisfaction of material things. The soul was the intellectual and moral aspect of the person — trained to recognize and understand virtue, whereby we can then apply this knowledge to daily living. Socrates examined knowledge, virtue, and wisdom in others, using the art of question and answer, to examine his fellow Athenians, and four hundred years later, Jesus used the same method to stimulate His listeners to think and search within for the truth of the answer. Socrates and Jesus were powerful teachers in their ability to expose false assumptions in order to lead their audiences to new thoughts, the illumination of new ideas, and the truth.

Socrates' conceptual beliefs and philosophical wisdom gives us insight for our growth as human beings. As we pursue the truth, we look to Jesus who provoked questions through His actions and holy words as the Holy Fathers' Vice Regent and in direct communication with God. Socrates and Christ taught virtue as a state of the soul that reflects our character and actions. For Socrates, virtue grew due to individual self-examination, and he acted as a mid-wife to initiate that process. Christ taught virtue as being in Him, and He brought us the power of the Holy Spirit as our teacher. Modern democracy is in need of wisdom's life giving force of spirit. Socrates was a secular philosopher; Christ is the sacred "Son of God" for believers. Our goal is an examination that will move us intellectually from Socrates — a philosopher who was born many centuries before Christ but felt close to the virtues during a superstitious era of polytheism — to the Holiness, truth, and wisdom of our Lord. Socrates' conceptual belief in the gods is not the path to our one true God — just as a conceptual belief in Christ, without dedication, trust, and obedience, does not warrant a bond with our Father. The Athenian logician adds many intellectual dimensions to our thinking; however, we clearly set things in the proper order: no philosopher is to be elevated above our belief in Christ. Our spirit holds a philosopher's ghost; whispering always whispering to think about freedom, eternal wisdom, philosophy, and now to think about God.

CHAPTER TWO

The Delphic Oracle: Socrates and Freedom

I often wonder if Socrates was alive today and walking through the streets and talking to our youth, if we would treat him to a cup of hemlock like the ancient Greeks. I can clearly envision him: clad in a thin and rumpled tunic, barefoot, a portly figure, somewhat rounded (but in good physical condition and healthy), and described by the ancients to be satyr-like and snub-nosed in his appearance. What we would notice first was his keen and observant eyes that protruded with intelligence (some ancients joked that he could see to the front and to the side — taking in everything at once!), framed by a round face that was centered by a broad and flat nose, and topped by a bald and somewhat large head. Socrates was charismatic and attracted a crowd wherever he went, and his contemporaries tell us about his charm, adding that he was pleasant and kind to everyone that he encountered. Ancient Athenian commercial and civic buildings were centered in the *agora* where citizens not only gathered to buy, sell, and barter goods, but also to talk about ideas. The master, Socrates, described himself as a mid-wife (*maieutic*) for the ideas of others, where his questions could bring out knowledge that lay dormant in the interlocutor's mind, and this knowledge could bear fruit. We know today that asking additional and more detailed questions can give us a personal understanding of ourselves, and a deeper and more thorough knowledge of our subject, and this comprehension can then lead to a greater personal autonomy. Socrates was interested in questioning and examining concepts: beauty, justice, goodness, virtue, courage, wisdom, and moderation. He was a philosopher, a lover of wisdom, and a teacher, but he did not teach in the ordinary way; he did not have a classroom or give lectures, nor write anything upon paper. We know Socrates through the words of Plato and the Platonic Dialogues, where he presents his master as the main interlocutor who uses dialectic to examine the beliefs of the Athenian youth.[7] Philosophical inquiry in the Platonic Dialogues takes on the form of a discourse where Socrates asks the questions and the respondent is pressed for a clearer idea of the concept. Through constant questioning, he examined the activities and opinions of the common citizens: shopkeepers, hucksters, metalworkers, scribes, horse trainers, and vineyard workers. He was interested in the opinions of every Athenian citizen and wherever he wandered, neighbors, colleagues, and the curious bystanders would join in because the gentle soul made them all feel important. Socrates valued the Athenian's answers to his questions, and — in turn — the Athenians found him to be kind to all classes. He smiled and joked, was polite to everyone and never got angry, and described himself as a gadfly who could sting the truth out of his subjects. Let us see if he can sting the truth out of us!

Socrates was a Greek thinker and teacher born in 469 B.C. in the deme Alopeke on the slopes of Mount Lycabettus — a short walk to Athens. He was put to death in 399 B.C. He was the son of Sophroniscus, a sculptor, and his mother, Phaenarete, a midwife. At the time of Socrates' birth, Athens was a cultural center and in the midst of celebrating victory over the Persians. Athenians were full of new ideas, which they expressed in philosophy, mathematics, plays, performances, rhetoric, oratory, the gymnasium, music, architecture, sculpture, and art. As a boy, he received a classical Greek education in music, gymnastics, and grammar, and he decided to become a sculptor like his father. Socrates married Xanthippe (described by the ancients as a shrew) and had three sons; two were still young when Athens put Socrates to death at the age of seventy. The only time that he left Athens was to serve honorably as a hoplite soldier in the Peloponnesian War (431 B.C.-404 B.C.). Socrates apprenticed to his father as a sculptor until one day — when he was a middle-aged man — Socrates' friend, Chaerephon, asked the Delphic oracle if any man was wiser than Socrates (Chaerephon put his question to the oracle approximately 430 B.C.). The Pythian priestess — seated on a tripod — would go into a trance and utter the God's (Apollo's) answer, which was then interpreted by an attending priest. The oracle replied, "No one is wiser" than Socrates! Thereafter, in the belief, he had no wisdom — Socrates set out on a questioning mission to find someone wiser than himself.

His examination of his fellow citizens and foreigners was the fulfillment of his divine mission. His wisdom was secular; his *daemon* or spiritual voice advised him on actions that he should not take. Socrates lived in an era of polytheism; however, at times he referred to "god" not "the gods". He was a model citizen, and Xenophon tells us that he sacrificed on both the public altars of the city and the private altar of his own home. Socrates studied with Archelaus (who was a student of Anaxagoras), and since Socrates wrote nothing, we learn about him through the pen of others: the pre-Socratic philosophers, Parmenides of Elea, his student Plato, Plato's student Aristotle, the playwright Aristophanes, the third-century A.D. biographer Diogenes Laertius, and the military general Xenophon. Philosophy began in ancient Greece, and we are the heirs today as modern "lovers of wisdom" — and we know that even a little philosophy is good for the soul.

Written on the temple of Apollo in Delphi were the words, *"gnothi seauton"*, "know thyself" — ancient advice that rings true to our modern ears. The religious cultures of ancient Athens and Rome are foreign practices to us, and yet we are enlightened by Socrates' philosophy and Jesus' divine teaching, so it is remarkable that they were both born in a pagan era. The ancient Greeks and Romans practiced the religion of their patron deity, and piety in worship was essential to the stability of the city: for Athens, the festival of Panathenaea and for Rome the festival of Lupercalia brought the citizen-body together in honor of the city's gods. The Panathenaic Games were held every four years beginning in 566 B.C. in Athens. The Games opened with a torch race from the Piraeus to the Acropolis (a tradition that is continued today with the opening ceremonies of our modern Olympics). One hundred oxen (*hekatombe*) were sacrificed to Athena, and the celebrants dined on the meat after the Games. The women devotedly sewed a special robe (the *peplos*) for the goddess, and she was carried as part of the procession. Athena's children honored their religion with athletic competitions, and cultural events — where the prize was awarded in a ceramic vessel that contained olive oil (*Panathenaic amphora*).

The Roman pastoral celebration Lupercalia — meant to bring fertility and health — was observed February 13th through the 15th near the cave of Lupercal on the Palatine Hill in honor of Lupa the she-wolf who suckled the infant orphan twins, Romulus and Remus, the founders of Rome. Their mother, Rhea Silvia, was forced to become a vestal virgin (priestess of the patron goddess of the earth, Vesta) by King Amulius (who had killed Rhea's father King Numitor). King Amulius wanted the twin brothers murdered but a servant rescued them and put them in a basket on the River Tiber. The brothers were rescued and suckled by a she-wolf (*lupa*), and fed by a woodpecker. During the festival of Lupercalia, the Luprci (young Roman men) would dress in the skins of the sacrificed goats and run along the walls of the old Palatine city. Young woman and girls would put out their hands to greet them, and their hands were struck by whips made from the skin of the animals. This spring pagan rite would avert evil spirits, purify the city, and ensure fertility for the Roman women.

Socrates admonished Athenians to care first and foremost for their souls. Socrates tells Phaedrus (an admirer of oratory) that for men who practice philosophy their souls grow their wings back, and they "are lifted up by justice to a place in heaven."[8] We follow Socrates if we do not want to be led by empty materialism, but seek a life based upon spiritual values, adherence to conscience, and the development of the soul. The Sophists criticized truth stating that it was an illusion and that everything was relative. Socrates criticized the Sophists for their philosophy — that focused on the investigation of nature — and for accepting payment for their skills. Although as a young man Socrates listened to the Sophists, his philosophy matured into the search for goodness and happiness. Socrates sought the truth through clear and consistent thinking with the goal of perfecting one's soul. In ancient Athens, the spoken word, *logos*, was a key to the life of the community. The classical Greeks liked to talk and spend an enormous time outside in the warm Mediterranean climate, discussing and questioning every issue that affected the Greek polis. In order to be heard or successful in politics, an Athenian needed rhetorical skills. There were no professional lawyers or judges, so winning a case before the democratic Assembly meant that you had oratory eloquence to sway the jurors. In the Classical Period of Greece (500-336 B.C.), Athens achieved its greatest political and cultural heights. Politics, religion, morality, athletics, and drama were on display within the Athenian polis. It is during this historical period that Plato founded his academy, the Lyceum, where we find the political leader Pericles, the building of the Parthenon on the Acropolis, and the Greek tragedies by Sophocles, Aeschylus, and Euripides.

The Golden City of Athens was unique as the birthplace of profound thinkers, the ideology of democracy, and freedom for the citizens. Through their intellectual achievements, the philosophers — Socrates (c. 469-399 B.C.), Plato (428/7-348/7 B.C.), and Aristotle (384-322 B.C.) — influenced western philosophical tradition. The philosophers found Athens' soil to be fertile ground for their freethinking ideas and exercises in the art of philosophy — fed by the perpetual access to new ideas, and the novel democratic society. The Athenians had a passion for the written and spoken word, while their neighbor, Sparta — who trained their youth for courageous battle and to die beautifully (*kalos thanatos*) on the battlefield — were suspicious of the written and spoken word (they did, however, find singing to be irresistible). The original meaning of the ancient philosophers' ideas can become scattered in time, i.e., what was meaningful and coherent in the past regarding phenomena can become incompatible given another time. Thankfully, their brilliance outshines any darkness we may encounter — their foresight still enlightens us today.

Plato was born in 427 B.C. into an aristocratic family on both his mother and father's side, and died at the age of eighty-one (347 B.C.). Plato (a nickname meaning "broad" and "strong" — whose real name was Aristocles) was wealthy, handsome, and had a superb physique. He was Socrates' remarkable student, teacher of the brilliant Aristotle, and prodigious writer of philosophical dialogues. Following Socrates' death in 399 B.C., Plato travelled to southern Italy and spent considerable time with the Pythagorean philosophical school. Upon his return to Athens, he founded the Academy in Athens (385 B.C.) — the first institution of higher learning in the western world. Located in the countryside near Athens and situated in the sacred groves of Acedemus, Plato spent the majority of his life there (except for his excursions to Syracuse) — teaching, writing and researching. His dialogues in the *Republic* teach us philosophy, logic, politics, ethics, rhetoric, mathematics, and religion. Plato tells us that he was a devoted follower of Socrates (*Apology*), and we hear the voice of Socrates in the Platonic dialogues. The Platonic idea of the immortality of the soul, the preexistence of souls, and that one's moral position determines one's accountability in the afterlife are positions that Plato holds, along with Socrates. Platonic philosophy taught that doing an injustice to another was far worse than suffering an abuse unjustly. Socrates teaches us to seek justice, piety, and virtue, which will bring an eternal advantage, because we will be better off in the next world. As we will discuss later in the *Republic*, the tripartite soul of the individual, i.e., the rational or logical, high-spirited, and appetitive parts of the soul will correspond to the three classes in society, i.e., the guardians, auxiliaries or soldiers, and the merchants living within Plato's city. The Platonic Theory of Forms holds that what makes an object beautiful is its association with absolute Beauty. There is a Form of Beauty, but this is not what beautiful things have in common, rather it is an exemplar — particular things somehow copy or "participate" in this Form of Beauty. The Forms exist "in the fullest sense"; they have a greater degree of reality than things in the empirical world; they are eternal and unchanging. The reality of the Forms is primary since everything else depends upon their existence.

Aristotle (384-322 B.C.) was born in the Macedonian city of Stagira, on the peninsula of Chalcidice (on the northern perimeter of Classical Greece). His father, Nicomachus, was the court physician to the Macedonian royal family. Aristotle was tutored privately until he was seventeen and joined Plato's Academy (368/7 B.C.), where he remained until the age of thirty-seven. After Plato died (348/7 B.C.), he spent five years in Asia Minor and Lesbos where he devoted some time to scientific and biological observation and research. Philip of Macedon invited Aristotle to tutor his son, Alexander the Great, in 343/2 B.C., an instruction that continued until Alexander was appointed regent for his father in 340 B.C. Then Aristotle returned to Athens, and established the Lyceum (335 B.C.), a program of study for all branches of inquiry that included ethics, aesthetics, logic, physics, biology, zoology, metaphysics, poetry and poetics, theatre, music, rhetoric, linguistics, politics, government, and science. Aristotle, who enjoyed walking while he lectured his students, was slight of build with small eyes, thinning hair (or bald), short beard, and was said to have spoken with a lisp. A majority of his writings (referred to as "a river of gold" by Cicero) are now lost, and we have only about one-third of the original works by Aristotle (in treatise form and thought to be lecture notes for his students). Like his teacher Plato, Aristotle aims at the universal, but unlike Plato, he finds the universal in particular things, which he calls the essence of things. Aristotle's views shifted from Platonism to empiricism, for example, Aristotle's epistemology (theory of knowledge) begins with a study of particular phenomena and rises to the knowledge of essences. Plato's epistemology begins with knowledge of universal Forms (or ideas) and descends to knowledge of particular imitations of these Forms. Like Socrates, Aristotle's metaphysical inquiry is dialectical, however, unlike Socrates, Aristotle postulates a theory of efficient and final causes. Four causes were used to explain everything: the material (out of which a thing comes to be); the formal (the essence, form or definition that is introduced by the efficient cause); the efficient (which produces the effect); and the final (the purpose for which a thing exists). God was the ultimate final cause, i.e., the Unmoved Mover, but unlike our Christian God, their god had no interest in the universe.

Aristotle was a great analyzer and categorizer, and his categories, e.g., biology, zoology, meteorology, metaphysics, and politics, are still used by us today. His systematic conception of logic is just one example of his important contributions in logic (*Prior Analytics*). Aristotle used inductive reasoning to create a universal process where we can learn everything conceivable about reality. The initial process of induction involved describing objects based on their characteristics, state of being, and actions. He described how we obtain information about objects through induction, deduction, and inference. Reasoning with a logical form, called a syllogism, was his invention and a basic unit of logic. If a=b and b=c, then a=c. Aristotle also pointed out the difference between *a priori* (knowledge that is independent of experience), and *a posteriori* reasoning (knowledge that is dependent on experience), and concludes from the particulars to the knowledge of the universal.

In the *Nicomachean Ethics,* Aristotle examines the Socratic question: how men should best live as a virtuous character (*ethike arête)* in order to have happiness (*eudaimonia),* the goal of life. Socrates believed that knowledge is virtue, and knowing the right thing to do will then lead one to make the correct choice. Aristotle believed that knowing what was right was not enough; one had to choose to act in the proper manner and form the habit of doing good. Aristotle believed that the good was happiness, which is an activity of the soul, which he divided into the rational and irrational part. For Aristotle, ethics was not just theoretical (where we contemplate good living), but also practical (where we actively create it). Our use of reason alone is a theoretical activity, but with the help of the appetitive and irrational part of the soul, we will be led to the practical aim of good living — the most admirable human activity. There are two types of virtue, the intellectual, and the moral, which correspond to the two parts of the soul.

Every virtue was a mean between two extremes, and the extremes are considered vices; for example, courage was a mean between cowardice and rashness. For Aristotle, the Golden Mean was excellence in activity where the individual uses moderation in all things to avoid extremes so that virtue in character is built by following the right habits.

Aristotle examined how justice aims at what is good in the *Politics,* and begins with the statement, "Man was by nature a political animal (*zoon politikon)*". It is only man that can make a communal community *(koinonia)* because he has the power of *logos*, i.e., speech, reason, and morality. The Greek *polis* was the highest form of community because it denotes "an association of free men" where the ruled were the rulers of the city — they formulated their own law codes, maintained an army, had their own system of government, and worshiped their own Olympian gods. Aristotle's conception of justice was different from our modern idea of equality; for him justice was the right proportion, so it would sometimes involve inequality. He taught that ethics was a branch of politics, and the magnanimous (great-souled) man would have every virtue, and therefore the better man deserves more. Humility is a trait that he considered a vice — it was the man with proper pride, who did not underestimate his own talents, whom Aristotle considered fit for ruling in either a monarchy or an aristocracy. He claimed that economic self-sufficiency *(autarkeia)* was the goal of each *polis*, self-supported by agriculture, hunting, and fishing. However, 5th century Athens was dependent on imports, with the exception of its silver, olives and olive oil, wine, honey and marble exports.

When Alexander the Great died in Babylon in 323 B.C. (after reigning for twelve years), Athens overthrew its Macedonian conquerors. Aristotle's connections to Macedonia and his philosophical activity brought him under suspicion, so he fled to Chalcis in Euboea where he died in 322 B.C. Aristotle remarked that he fled so that Athens could not sin twice against philosophy. Aristotle's influence on Western and Eastern thought in philosophy, logic, ethics, humanities, and science is as influential as Plato and Socrates' enduring legacy.

Draco was the first legislator of Athens (7th century B.C.), and he replaced the oral law by a written code that is known for its Draconian harshness. Draco invented the Council of Four Hundred, where free men elected the members from among themselves. Before the democratic system was born, archons or chief magistrates, and the Areopagus (made up of ex-archons) ruled Athens. These members were primarily aristocrats who ruled for their own advantage. By the 6th century B.C., the rich ruled, and the common people called upon Solon (638 B.C.-558 B.C.), the chief archon at the time, to liberate them. Athens at this time was a society primarily made up of independent farmers who had lost their land holdings to creditors, and had become enslaved because of debt-bondage. This social crisis led to social and political unrest, and the people elected Solon as head archon in 594 B.C., to reform the Draconian laws that had forced debtors into slavery. Solon's reforms repealed Draco's harshly written edicts (except for the homicide directive), healed the division between the rich and the poor, established new courts, and created a polis where the people could rationally and peacefully settle their various conflicts.

Thirty-three years after Solon's reign of compromise, Peisistratos made himself tyrant ruler over Athens between 561 and 527 B.C., by gaining support of the poor and his bodyguards. (Our modern connotation of a tyrant is a single ruler, often repressive and violent — Peisistratos' rule was by personal ability even though he took his position in violation of the Greek tradition, for he was an autocrat who seized power illegitimately.) Peisistratos established a revolving loan for peasants, so the middle and lower classes could keep possession of their property, and established "deme-judges" who went on circuit and exercised their judicial powers. (A deme was a geographical unit of local government.) After the expulsion of the Peisistratids (Peisistratos, and his two sons, Hipparchus and Hippias, who ruled Athens from 546 to 510 B.C.), political conflict was heightened by the presence of Spartan military forces in Athens.

Athenian democracy flourished around the fifth century B.C., and Solon (594 B.C.), Cleisthenes (508/7 B.C.), Ephialtes (462 B.C.), and Pericles (461 B.C.) contributed much to the development of Athenian democracy. Solon was a lawgiver and a poet, and considered by the Athenians to be a wise (*sophos*) man. However, he was an oligarch who believed that rule was by the few and the aristocrats controlled the political life. The reforms of Cleisthenes in 508/7 B.C., removed the domination of the aristocratic families from the city's rule. Cleisthenes welcomed the *hoi poloi* (ordinary people) into his circle in order to obtain power, and the first direct democracy was born. The word "democracy" (*demokratia*) combines *demos*, which means "people" and refers to the entire citizen body, with *kratos*, which means "force" or "power". The Athenian Assembly and the Areopagus were of ancient origin (made up of the old aristocracy), and the Aereopagus Council was made up of nine Archons whose membership was restricted to the wealthy property classes. Cleisthenes formed the new Council of Five Hundred made up yearly of fifty members from the tribes that Cleisthenes created to represent local political loyalties instead of the status of the aristocracy. After 487 B.C., lot chose the Archons from the five hundred candidates that were selected by the local demes. Pericles' mentor, Ephialtes, removed power from the Aereopagus in 462 B.C., and was assassinated a few months later. During this same period, the property qualifications for holding office were lowered, and a compensation for serving on the Council and in the courts was established (possibly in 429 B.C.). Any male citizen — who was at least eighteen years old — could speak and vote in the assembly. The good orators could easily sway the crowd and dominate the political agenda, like the Sophist Gorgias, who taught the art of public speaking. Socrates questions him in Plato's Gorgias about the nature and power of his craft to persuade people and juries about what is good and right.

Pericles of Chorlargeus (495 B.C.-430 B.C.) was the son of the politician Xanthippus, and was born into the powerful Alcmaeonid family on his mother's side. Pericles — the most prominent and influential Greek statesman, an accomplished *rhetor* or orator, general (*strategos)*, and the longest lasting democratic leader — came to power in Athens in 461 B.C. The period during which he led Athens (approximately 461-429 B.C.), was known as the "Age of Pericles" and it was a time when we find the historical Socrates — ill-clad, barefoot, and listening to his oracle or *daimon* (what Christians would call the voice of conscience, and remember that St. Joan of Arc was inspired by heavenly voices!). Guided by Pericles and under the influence of victory and wealth, Athens had a remarkable period of cultural growth. He shaped and promoted democracy — intellectually, theoretically, and strategically — through the arts, music, literature, education, culture, and architecture. He was, for example, the mastermind behind the building of the Acropolis, (whose architecture was burned down by the Persians). This included the Parthenon (begun in 447 B.C. and completed in 432 B.C.), the Propylaea (the entrance hall to the summit of the Acropolis), the temple to Hephaestus, the temple to Nemesis (goddess of fate), Odeon concert-hall (440 B.C.), and the golden statue of Athena sculpted by his friend Phidias.

The Age of Pericles was a glorious time for Athens where we find the Greek tragedians Aeschylus, Sophocles, and Euripides, and the father of historians, Herodotus. Socrates, Plato, Anaxagoras, Protagoras, and the Sophists (who taught the young men the art of disputation and rhetoric for a fee) were occupied with philosophical questions. Pericles' military accomplishments were the center of his power, where he gained respect along with his intellectual and rhetorical talents, and his incorruptible virtue. For over twenty years, he led many military expeditions — primarily cautious naval battles because he believed that the Peloponnesians were unbeatable on the land. He rebuilt the walls of Athens to protect her from the Spartans. Pericles strategy was to preserve the empire, not expansion. By the late 5th century, Athenian cultural practice honored those who had died in war (to bolster up their new democracy) by holding a public funeral over which a prominent citizen presided with a speech. From Pericles' Funeral Oration (a famous speech from Thucydides' *History of the Peloponnesian War*), we can identify the goals of Athenian democracy: *demokratia* (democracy), *eleutheria* (freedom), *isonomia* (equality), *dike* (justice) and *parrhesia* (free speech).[9] The funeral oration was a eulogy of the war-dead, a glorification of Athenian achievements and her commitment to democracy and freedom, and designed to stir the spirits of the Athenians at wartime.

Five years after Pericles divorced his wife (445 B.C. — the name of his first wife is unknown), Aspasia (470-400 B.C.) became his mistress and consort until the end of his life. Born in the Ionian Greek city of Miletus, Aspasia was a beautiful and exceptional Greek woman who was educated — literate and well read — and mentioned in the philosophical writings of Plato, Xenophon, Aeschines, and Antisthenes. There are conflicting stories about Aspasia's life, and some scholars have suggested that she was a *hetaera* (harlot) and operated a brothel. Socrates knew Aspasia well — Plato tells us that she was a tutor in rhetoric to Socrates[10] — and he recites Aspasia's speech for the dead in *Menexenus*, "We ought to remember and praise those men forever, because by their valor we won not only that naval engagement, but also the rest of the war."[11] Socrates argued that women should play a much larger role in Athenian society, and receive the same education as males. Socrates, for example, recommended Aspasia as a master to teach rhetoric to the wealthy young male Athenians. Although the relationship between Pericles and Aspasia caused scandal in male-dominated Athens, Pericles treated Aspasia as an equal. In ancient Athens, male citizens were equal before the law, (exceptions were women, slaves, and foreign residents), where every citizen could participate in the public democratic sphere: vote in the Assembly, serve on the Council of Five Hundred, and act as a juror. The traditional cultural conventions of Athens required the citizens to respect parents, be hospitable to strangers, and give a proper burial to the dead.

Throughout the sixth and fifth centuries B.C., the Greeks were overrun and occupied by the powerful, land-hungry Persians. When the Persian forces were defeated at the Battle of Salamis (fought in September 480 B.C.) and Plataea (fought in August 479 B.C.), and the Hellenic victory at the Eurymedon River (466 B.C.), Athens abandoned her alliance with Sparta (they had originally fought as allies in the Greco-Persian Wars). The ancient city-state had suffered from numerous conflicts, so her triumph under the newly formed democracy was celebrated by a city designed to show off this fledgling government. The Athenians transformed their city to house the new democratic system. The Assembly of Athens met once a month (and sometimes up to three times per month) on Pynx hill in a space that could hold up to 6,000 citizens. Citizens who had the right to vote and speak in the Assembly, were adult males (both parents also had to be citizens), eighteen years of age or older, who had completed military training as *ephebes*. In 430 B.C., out of a population of about 230,000 (including slaves) the male citizenship would number between 30,000 to 50,000. Each participating citizen voted directly on legislation and executive bills. In 594 B.C., Solon had set up the *boule* of 400 (consisting of 100 members from each of the four tribes and elected by lot every year) to prepare the agenda and guide the work for the Assembly or *Ecclesia*. The law was the outcome of a vote in the Assembly, where ordinary citizens were chosen at random for a term of one month. These citizens lived at state expense in a circular building called the *Prytaneion* adjacent to the *bouleuterion*, where the *boule* met. The law courts (*dikasterion*) — where large juries made decisions — were important to the process of democratization, and the decision of the Assembly could be challenged by the law courts. The law was devised and enforced by magistrates (*archai*) — all citizens were eligible for a position that had limited terms of office with no re-election. Athenians knew that the rulers would then become the ruled. Administrative decisions were made by boards of officials who were chosen by lot for short-term service that required free time and personal finances that the officials used to fund municipal projects that were vital to the society, for example, festivals, and building ships.

Ten generals (*strategoi*) were elected each year (one from each tribe) and their position was one of political power. When we look at the list of generals we also see men who led Athens not just in strength and power during warfare, but were also outstanding in charisma, strategy and politics — Themistocles, Cimon, Nicias, Alcibiades, Cleon, and of course, Pericles (who was elected *strategos* every year from 443 B.C. until his death in 429 B.C.). The generals also held public office, and could influence the agenda of the Assembly for their own personal causes.

At Lyreum, in 483 B.C., the Athenians struck a giant deposit of lead that contained precious particles of silver. This wealth contributed to the realization of Themistocles' (524-459 B.C.) vision of an Athens that would command the sea by building the 200 triremes (483 B.C.) that would protect Athens from subsequent Persian invasions. These triremes were among the thirty ships with 1,000 hoplite soldiers that sailed north to Potidaea — a colony of Corinth — in 432 B.C. to repeal a revolt by the Potidaeans (who wanted to assert their autonomy). Athens had increased the annual levy from six to fifteen talents, ordered the Potidaeans to pull down their walls, send hostages to Athens, expel Corinthian ambassadors, and sever connections with Corinth. At stake for Athens was the fertile rich territory of Potidaea that brought cash, iron, and an expansion of the Athenian empire — democracy and culture. Socrates fought courageously as a hoplite soldier at Potidaea (his first engagement in 432 B.C.), at Delium (424 B.C.), and his last engagement was when he was forty-eight at Amphipolis. Socrates would have had two years military training in his early twenties, and as a hoplite soldier, his body was protected by a shield and body armor, and he was trained to fight with a spear. The victorious Athenian army was on its way home when they were ambushed near Spartolos. In the *Symposium,* Alcibiades tells the Symposium audience how Socrates singlehandedly saved his life and his weapons when he was wounded at Potidaea.[12]

After Pericles death in 429 B.C., Athens was ruled by a series of oligarchs who had gained their wealth from commerce or trade (*neoploutus*). Toward the end of the Peloponnesian War (431-404 B.C.), the Athenian democracy was interrupted twice by oligarchic revolutions. In 415 B.C., Athens was preparing her ships to sail for a controversial invasion of Sicily (to ensure that the Athenian route for supplies was secure), when all of the city's Hermes were mutilated. (Hermes were rough statues of the face and phallus of Hermes — the god of travel — that marked the boundaries of homes from public places.) Many prominent Athenians were charged with crimes of impiety (*asebeia*) including Alcibiades III, a wealthy member of the Alcmaeonid family who had been orphaned at age six, reared by Pericles, and a student of Socrates. He was a unique product of the Greek exceptionalism — wealthy, handsome, a charming statesman, general (strategos), and orator. Alcibiades and his friends were also accused of a staged initiation rite of the Eleusinian mysteries, where Alcibiades reportedly acted as high priest. The accused men fled into exile where they were condemned of the sacrilege *in absentio,* and their property was confiscated and sold by the state. Alcibiades III had planned the controversial Sicilian expedition and, although, he asked for a trial to prove his innocence, he was forced by his enemies to set sail for Sicily with the charges unresolved. He was recalled from the Sicilian invasion to stand trial, but he escaped while being escorted back to Athens, and defected to Sparta where he served as a military advisor.[13] For twelve months, the rule of the Thirty Tyrants (404 B.C. through 403 B.C.) led by Critias IV, traumatized the city by purging it of political enemies. These legally elected oligarchs were pro-Spartan juntas whose death squads roamed the streets of Athens to kill their rivals by numerous gruesome slaughters that included a perfected dose of death by hemlock. The oligarchs murdered between 1,000 and 1,500 Athenians, and many citizens went into exile. They also ordered Socrates to bring in Leon from Salamis (so he could be executed), however, Socrates refused. Socrates relates the past events in the *Apology,* "They gave many such orders to many people in order to implicate as many as possible in their guilt. Then I showed again, not in words but in action, that, if it were not rather vulgar to say so, death is something I couldn't care less about, but that my whole concern is not to do anything unjust or impious. That government, powerful as it was, did not frighten me into any wrongdoing. When we left the Hall, the other four went to Salamis and brought in Leon, but I went home. I might have been put to death for this, had not that government fallen shortly afterwards. There are many who will witness to these events."[14]

Athenian democracy was restored in 403 B.C. — a potent time when Athens' direct democracy was discussed and debated, and the power of persuasion (*peitho*) was used to stir men's thoughts for the collective freedom of the polis. Socrates' political vision was an ethical pursuit, where he believed that the state should place ethics above power and wealth. Socrates practiced a systematic form of interrogation to discover if his interlocutors knew what they professed to know, and whether or not they agreed to the Socratic moral position that takes virtue seriously. Some of the questions that Socrates asked: what are justice (*dikeosyni*), virtue (*arête*), moderation (*sophrosune*), courage (*andreia*), good (*agathos*), and piety (*eusebeia*)? Socrates' search for *arête*, excellence, had a moral purpose. Whenever the youth gathered around him and asked his advice on matters of conduct, Socrates' questions opened up the heart and soul of those being examined, his voice smoothed over the listener's soul as both a balm to heal and an herb to invigorate. Those who listened to him remembered the sealed treasures in their own souls and then, following the masters lead, would look into their own to discover the concealed wisdom hidden there. The Socratic questions of how we ought to live, and how do we have knowledge of the virtue that leads to happiness as we live the right way, are questions that we continue to ask ourselves today. We are like the ancient Athenians because we are also questioning beings living in a democratic society of freedom seekers;

however, unlike Athena's children, we have somehow lost our way through a cloud of empty materialistic pursuits.

Socrates said to Alcibiades (who was known to be ambitious), "So the command that we should know ourselves means that we should know our souls".[15] The salvation of our great nation does not rely on power politics but on the awakening power of the exceptional high-souled spirit. The spirit of our modern time is rooted in the knowledge and wisdom of the great thinkers of the past; and these thinkers step forward now to instruct us in an ethical political vision, (like Socrates' vision, that suits everyone because its foundation is based upon truth). Socrates' voice is the oratory of one who has wisdom, knowledge, and truth. Our modern democracy — as an ideal — is a democracy of individual freedom for everyone, and we all have a yearning and perception of this expansive freedom. Freedom is the most delicious nourishment offered to refresh humankind, and it must necessarily — as food for the life of the soul — be available to everyone. As ancient Athens built a new democracy, Socrates urged his fellow Athenians to become acquainted with their souls; as America refreshes its democracy, we learn to follow the Socratic spirit and look within to discover our true nature — our souls — so that we can genuinely participate in democracy and freedom.

Socrates — humble, down-to-earth, and beloved — was an influence on his contemporaries and his philosophy has grown in stature throughout history. Plato, one of Socrates most beloved disciples, gives us our picture of him through the pages of the Platonic dialogues. Socrates' ideas were complex, and his influence on philosophy included diverse thinkers like Antisthenes, the founder of the Cynic school, the school of Stoicism, Aristippus, the founder of the Cyrenaica school, and Euclides, the founder of the Megarian school, known for dialectics. It is said that when one of Socrates' friends, Chaerephon, asked the Delphic Oracle to name the wisest person in Greece, the Oracle replied that it was Socrates. This inspired a life-long search by the philosopher to find the wisest person in Greece, and Socrates concluded that his own wisdom meant that he knew nothing, and he was conscious of his own ignorance. The word philosophia was coined by the Greeks, and means "love of wisdom". He taught us that philosophy is not an activity done in isolation but amongst a community of thinkers, and is an exercise for wisdom. Philosophy does not spring out of our brain as an inspiration from Minerva, but is an exercise for seekers who hope to improve their lives, add enlightenment to their communities, grow their spirituality, enhance harmony and equality, attract love to their human design, and make spiritual progress. Socrates would tell us that philosophy is not just a theoretical exercise but is the choice of a way of life and living, and a preparation for wisdom, even if we never actually become wise. He continued to move toward the good, and he saw that his contemporaries also arrived at knowledge of the good as they endured the Socratic *catharsis*.

The love of knowledge sends us on a quest that fills the void in our soul. The knowledge of philosophy speaks to us through the voice of the soul, and we know that even a little bit of philosophy is good for us. On our own personal and humble journey, we would like to invoke Lady Philosophy to guide us as we join Socrates by the River Ilissos. The Athenians washed in the water of this sacred River whenever they had free time. Lady Philosophy, the first soul of creative ideas, we see your beauty in our mind's eye and our desire to behold your treasure leads us to strive for purer thoughts that honor philosophy. Lady Philosophy, one of the Queens of Heaven, hold out your golden basket of jewels so that we may possess just one small purple gem of wisdom. May our wisdom run deep like that ancient and sacred River Ilissos and may our passions guard and strengthen our soul.

We are all philosophers because we all have opinions, world-views, and inquisitive and questioning natures. We are all God's children and children of the Light. Like the analogy in Plato's Cave, we are temporarily chained in the darkness — and seeing only shadows of the real things — waiting for our ascent into the light so that we may see and understand real things, and not the imitation of things. We compartmentalize our experiences and listen somewhat and sometimes to our inner voice for guidance. Socrates teaches us to listen wholeheartedly to our inner intuitive voice. His wisdom was secular; his *daemon* or spiritual voice advised him, but only in actions that he should not take. The Holy Bible teaches us about God's love, His commandments, and the wisdom of Christ's teachings so that we may understand the sacred realm and trust the Holy Spirit who guides us.

The ancient Greeks had an oral tradition (a method of keeping a culture alive without depending on the written word) for their habit was to read aloud. Socrates was often critical of the Sophists, who were only concerned with speechifying and did not know how to lead a discussion.[16] Unlike the Sophists, he never charged fees for speaking engagements or teaching, which he characterized as his art of conversing. When engaged in dialog, he forced the individual to stick to the subject, and obliged them to examine the complexities of an argument by leading them to abstract abbreviations of the topic. He usually began his conversations at the periphery of the subject, and then like a magician, he wound his golden words around the topic to bring the matter to the heart of the truth. The philosopher's intention was not to develop a discourse that was an end in itself, but to utilize a dialog that would have a profound effect on the individual, and subsequently their soul. Socrates wanted people to understand how to interpret and reinterpret knowledge, eventually gaining insight into their beliefs. His aim was not just the definition of what was in question, but felt that examination would lead to moral reform. The wise teacher thought that *elenchus* would lead to happier and more virtuous individuals.

As a citizen, his character was just and he behaved with dignity and virtue in everything that he did. For Socrates, an unexamined life was not worth living;[17] He needed to examine himself and others, for an honorable individual always aimed at improving their actions and never harming anyone. His mission focused on truth, wisdom, and the care and perfection of the soul.[18] Each soul must possess its own virtue and its function was to manage and rule over itself; an ordered soul has a goal of virtuous action.

Socrates cultivated and practiced equanimity, i.e., mind-fullness or being present with his fellow Athenians. He embodied wisdom, compassion, and loving-kindness as he practiced the art of dialectic with others. His followers were all treated impartially as they grew together in a clarity of vision of the Platonic ideas. Socrates' super natural voice gave him an unobstructed vision that was perceived by others to be a spiritual communion with the gods. The mentor, for example, claimed to learn the nature of love from the Goddess Diotima, poetic knowledge that Socrates shared with his fellow banqueters in the *Symposium*.[19] The act of beginning a dialogue with him opened with an exchange of questions and answers that would produce profound results. His sacred mission led to a widening of the soul's apertures, where a deep creative understanding would flow out of the activity. Socrates' courageousness of heart was extended as empathy toward the thoughts of others. An encounter with him was a magical moment for the Athenian youth, who were attracted to the Master due to the goodness of his heart and spirit, and an exchange with him would leave them with a fresh, unique, and creative way of thinking.

The sage did not teach us what to think but he taught us *how* to think. If our spirit resides with him what allegiance can we hold for a materialistic America, whose citizens would (if they discovered a modern Socrates rambling about the marketplace, disturbing their ideas), probably vote a fate for him no better than the one given to him by the Ancient Greeks. America may not be ready for Socrates and Socratic philosophy, but she is now ready for true freedom: that freedom which begins as an axiological idea but ends with true and effective functioning of the individual's natural talents. Let us, philosophically define natural as that element which is essential to a particular mode of being. Axiological ideas are those that are fundamental to our existence as human beings and enable us to identify the values that influence our perceptions, decisions, and deeds. Axiology is derived from two Greek words: *axios* (worth or value) and *logos* (logic, theory or reasoning) and is the theory of value. For example, there is a necessary connection between the idea of individual freedom and democratic rule. These fundamentals are the framework for our patterns of thinking, as we utilize these ideas for subsequent cognate notions. Socrates' philosophy is freeing because he teaches us the methods of cross-examination and refutation (elenchus), and inductive reasoning — forcing us to re-examine our beliefs.

His methodology can assist western Christianity, as we seek and discover new paths to God and freedom. The general body of Americans can remember when brother could trust brother, to be an American was an honor and a virtue, a man or woman's handshake was their word, and our nation was the light of freedom for the world. We will again become familiar with Socratic philosophy — and Christian teaching — that reminds us that spirit is necessary for the maturity of our country. Our democratic aspirations will lead us to take our loftiest achievement and enliven it with the rational and spiritual ideas within its walls. Democracy needs no dogma (the dogma has already been promulgated) however, it requires a strength of mind. The spirit of freedom is upon the earth, and a covenant of hope and desire will bind the material world to the spiritual for an embodiment of personal liberty within this great nation. We are adept in our pursuit of material things, however, it has not brought us fulfillment. We have now matured in our understanding of what gives us true happiness, and this contentment lies in our personal autonomy.

A religious identity builds over time through a whole life of study, worship, learning, obedience, reason, passion, heart, and soul where we see that we are not one-dimensional creatures but four-dimensional, and our personality erupts in the understanding of our divine nature. Our classroom is made up of matter and material objects, but also ideas that strengthen our soul's capacity for becoming free. These ideas of freedom are summarized as freedom of self, freedom of intellect, freedom of movement, and freedom of ratiocination or reason. These ideas of freedom make up the dimensions necessary for a free self, that is, the width, length and height, or breadth of time and space that will assist in regenerating a material body into a spiritual one. We are in need of spiritual nourishment "and not holding fast to the head, from whom the entire body, being supplied and held together by the joints and ligaments, grows with a growth which is from God" (Col 2:19). Our vision of the Glorious Body of Christ — Soul and Spirit, Powers, Glorious Nature, Divine Nature and His Holy Attributes — feeds and sustains our spiritual hunger. We have outgrown our youth but remaining childlike in our trust — and now as adults within this truth, we want to exercise our maturity as free beings in Christ within a free nation. Our prayer is that our nation will return to God — the belief relished by our nation's Founding Fathers — and our obedience will soon bring God's protective spirit back over the nation.

Like Socrates, we strive for wisdom but humbly make no claims to being wise. More important to us than our gaining Socratic wisdom, is our kinship for God's Kingdom, and He rules us for spiritual growth not material prosperity, however, any material prosperity that we do gain is for His greater glory. We learn obedience to God's governance over us because this leads to our dependence upon Him for our natural growth as our true being is in His spirit. "Cease striving and know that I am God; I will be exalted among the nations, I will be exalted in the earth" (Psalms 46:10). The indwelling of Jesus in our hearts is our conformity to God's rule, and we develop Christ's love toward others, gentleness, loving-kindness, charity, patience, and purity. When God commands us "to go", we must obey and "go", not claim a prideful right to our own inclinations or argue that it is not the right time, or assert that we are not properly prepared. The Apostle John writes, "That which is born of the flesh is flesh, and that which is born of the Spirit is spirit. Do not be amazed that I said to you, 'You must be born again' " (John 3:6-7). We think about Socrates, who took the cup of hemlock with courage and calmness, and we reflect on what more we can do, as Christians, with certainty of the afterlife that Socrates (who lived before Christ) also believed in. We go forward with a special determination to accomplish what God sets out for us.

In the Age of Freedom, we are independent — independent of one another, yet dependent upon the sound ideas of prior thinkers to strengthen and expand our individual freedom. We turn to past masters to learn from their vision on how we should lay our personal foundation in freedom. A formula for success in this mission is to follow the Socratic quest for individual excellence. Socrates taught that we see through the glass darkly, and therefore do not yet understand that we are nourished through the viscosity of God's nutritive Good. Individual thinkers who view life Socratically — as a dialectical exercise — are likely to throw off the bonds of the known and strike out into new territory that will lead them to spiritual freedom. Some of the questions that we wish to explore are — what predominant ideas hold us together as a nation? How do we understand these thoughts and how do these relate to the concept of freedom for the individual, community, city, state, and our country? In addition, we want to examine the Platonic Forms (ideals) and ask if there is a Form of Beauty and a Form of Goodness, for what use is a beautiful Form unless there are good souls to envision it. What use can be made of a good city, if there are no good souls to populate it? Today, the sphere of human knowledge is vast — calling for clarity and expansion — and new ideas are put forth in every discipline. That extraordinary character, Socrates, who strutted like a peacock but spoke like a sage, can give us intellectual offspring in time — even today. Moreover, we pray that Christ will shepherd our offspring into the proper spiritual maturity.

A philosopher or philosophy-minded individual can see distinguishing marks of liberation in the new territory. Our personal creative and imaginative energy can carry us forward and do much for our progress in discovering new ideas. Each independent person is qualified to assist in our progress toward a model commonwealth; our own free nature is the ultimate source of our collective freedom, and our unrestricted activity within the community will assist us in defining a good city. The Aristotelian man has an intrinsic sense of justice, which by necessity is exercised within a community of justice-bearing men and woman. Similarly, the Socratic men and women have a rational and innate sense of what is just and unjust, and make up the good city. We discover our free self through philosophy and religion, and are also exercising and learning more about our own personal freedom. We are born free, but do not fully partake of this freedom until our meditations become coextensive with our actions. All reformation is a canonical promotion of the free self, and that which reclaims being is the activity of unrestricted citizens living together within a good city. Plato teaches us that these eternal archetypes are seen through our intellectual tools of logic, mathematics, and symbolism. The world of the Platonic intelligence is a spiritual world where our reasoning can transcend time and space. Reason is not just an analytical power, but is also a powerful creative tool for discovering additional ideas.

"There is a river whose streams make glad the city of God, The holy dwelling places of the Host High. God is in the midst of her, she will not be moved" (Psalms 46:4-5). The gentle Jesus taught us that we know little of the holy love that God has for us; following His Holy Spirit, we learn to open our hearts to Him, ensuing faithfully in obedience.

Jesus and Socrates' teachings parallel for they both speak how the soul is nourished through its human growth and understanding of that which is holy. As human beings, we are naturally attracted to the spiritually radiant mental light where we discover the illumination of truth. Jesus taught us, "By your endurance you will gain your lives" (Luke 21:19). Through Christ's Holiness, our hearts are healed, guarded, searched, and perfected in that image that God has created for us. The divinity in Christ shines on us — by His light, we understand that which is good. The wisdom that we seek to emulate is based on the laws of God, which is the wisdom of the heavens. The cumulative acumen of philosophy (earthly knowledge) is there for the benefit of all, for Socrates has illuminated a creative receptacle for conscious beings as a source for our own goodness. We do not read Plato as we read Holy Writ, but we read for an understanding and clarity of vision that stimulates reason and an understanding of our moral direction. This quest for the understanding of profound ideals leads to a devotion to God. Philosophy teaches the human being the meaning of worship by putting it into actuality, with singleness of heart and purity of service, the content of our study is put into form, that is, figure and intuition are put into active service on behalf of God's mission for us.

Philosophy is but a shadow of the divine, so our understanding of the Platonic Forms leads us on the road to instruction and prayers. These immaterial archetypes (i.e. the soul) are models that all else emulates in life. The Platonic Form of the Good is at the top of the hierarchy, illuminating all the Forms below it. In the Republic, Plato uses the metaphor of the sun that illuminates objects in the visible realm. Our attention to the Platonic Forms brings our thinking into focus so that we may uncover a deeper reality that is the Beauty of God's realm. Socrates believed that the true self is not the body, but the inner beauty of the soul, and happiness (eudaimonia) was gained through the goodness of its inner qualities. As Christian children, we have beautiful souls and generate a moral happiness by living a Christian life. Innately structured to be in spiritual communion with God, we give the Glory to Him. "I was hungry, and you gave Me something to eat; I was thirsty, and you gave Me something to drink; I was a stranger, and you invited Me in; naked and you clothed Me; I was sick, and you visited me..." (Mat 25:35-36). Christ fills all in all in the universe, and we are His emissaries on earth. "He has made everything appropriate in its time. He has also set eternity in their heart, yet so that man will not find out the work which God has done from the beginning even to the end" (Eccl 3:11).

As God's children, we are born free; this freedom is properly exercised when our activities take place among other freedom-seeking people. Freedom becomes substantial and workable when it arises from within the receptacle of individuality, and is then exercised within the community, not vice versa. We only truly understand that idea which we take up personally, either in time in the initiation of action or in a space of perpetual activity, or activity for the sake of clarifying a preexisting mental experiment. Abstract thinking alone will not accomplish the making of the best of possible cities for us, because you can push an abstract thought process to the extreme, but until you experiment with your idea within the material world, you will not know if it is a workable concept or not. Therefore, freedom is not just an abstract concept or a theoretical construction, but becomes an active force when the replication of ideas of the free individual are constructed within space-time.

The principle of freedom is alive in the heart, soul, and mind of a free individual prior to its extension in a societal class. Each free individual has a unique function, as does the community, but where they are similar is in the goal toward which they both seek, varying in degree but not in kind (that is, meaningful as far as the consciousness of the individual is concerned). This goal is always freedom. Freedom is the natural heritage of humankind and is the progressive goal of the community. So in order to maintain this heritage and to achieve our objectives, we adhere individually to Socratic ethics, and collectively to an understanding of axiological ideas — thoughts that are the basis to our existence as human beings. There is a fundamental symmetry between the involution of axiological ideas and the spiritual advancement of human beings. This connection is strengthened or weakened by the trial of thoughts as we examine possible activities and determine if the act is symmetrical with the idea, and if the wealth of the concept can be properly proved in activity. Is there a necessary connection between individual freedom and democratic rule? Does he/she who governs interfere with our autonomous being? If we define the idea of freedom as an axiological one, then we see this archetype in the Constitution of the United States, the foundation for autonomy. There are numerous motives and rewards to the human being who searches for and deploys these theories: personal growth and potential, actualization of the soul or power (*dunamis*), wisdom (*sophia*), knowledge (*episteme*), moral and spiritual understanding and development, pleasure, happiness (eudaimonia*)*, curiosity, intellectual comprehension, survival, and enhancement of the community, to name just a few of the advantages.

The holy benefit is to participate freely in God's redemptive time. We are nourished by a Mind that is holy and exalted, and we may speculate that this Sacred Mind utilizes axiological ideas that are eternal. Our human and earthly covenant is to imitate (to the degree humanly possible) the divine beauty of these fundamental thoughts. God is outside of time, i.e., eternal and infinite, and these eternal concepts are veiled to us; we strive (in goodness) to touch the periphery of redemptive time and to place our feet firmly in God's camp. Redemption (*agorazo*) in ancient Greece meant, "to purchase in the marketplace". Christ's blood released us from sin and bondage to a renewed life in Him. Our job is regeneration as God's creatures, because "in Him we have redemption through His blood, the forgiveness of our trespasses, according to the richness of his grace which He lavished on us. In all wisdom and insight" (Eph 1:7-8).

Individuals educated in philosophy strive for moral and spiritual knowledge, and desire to understand how the philosophy of ideas will relate to the individual and the community. This knowledge of ideas is freeing because the ability to express our thoughts — is freedom from fear. Natan Sharansky writes, "In America, for instance, freedom of speech and religion are considered sacrosanct." (See Natan Sharansky, The Case for Democracy: The Power of Freedom to Overcome Tyranny and Terror, p. 39.) The Socratic search for clarity of ideas and definitions assists us as we discover that knowledge of the definition of an object was necessary prior to the application of the idea in the practical realm. An example of this Socratic method is taught in the Republic in the Euthyphro where Socrates searches for a definition of piety. We cannot understand a pious act without first obtaining its correct definition. Thus, it serves a practical function because once we deliberate about an object; we can then apply this knowledge to test the morality (or "rightness") and our course of action.

Socratic philosophy is relevant to our growth as individuals, and for an understanding of our place within our community. The Socratic arguments examine not only the definition of the ideas or concepts, but also individual's actions that determine the consequences of how people live amongst themselves. As citizens of a democracy, we take to heart our principles of individual freedom. The greatest lessons of democracy are to be found in the ideas that are contiguous with freedom, i.e., justice and liberty — concepts which we will examine later. The democratic republican principle is one of freedom, and the transcendental engagement of this axiom will bring us to a discovery of what we can create for an excellent, spiritual, and good society. The immortal giants of ancient Greece stride over our nation and imprint our society with genius and determination, and help us to learn that we should no longer place our reliance upon materialism, because democracy is dead without the life-giving force of spirit. The past masters are the harbingers of the good news of God's Holy Hand on our nation.

Although Socrates was born in a superstitious era, he rode the crest of reason above the Dionysian and Orphic cults. The ancient Pythagoreans held the belief that each sphere of the universe produced a note as it revolved around the earth and the harmonious whole was called the "music of the spheres". Socrates teaches Glaucon (Plato's brother) what our souls will experience after death, "And up above on each of the rims of the circles stood a Siren, uttering a single sound, one single note. And the concord of the eight notes produces a single harmony. And there were three other beings sitting at equal distances from one another, each on a throne.... They were dressed in white, with garlands on their heads, and they sang to the music of the sirens."[20] This melodious sound of the singing of the celestial sirens is unheard since the Fall of Adam and Eve, but a sinless person might be blessed to hear it — perhaps Socrates was such a man!

The Socratic spirit was human and his reason (*eusebes logismos*, i.e., pious reason) was devout; he battled dead philosophy. Socrates was seventy years old in 399 B.C. when he was indicted for breaking the law for 'impiety' for offending the Olympian gods, and corruption of the youth. (Meletus the poet, Anytus the craftsman, and Lycon the politician brought the charges against Him.) He defended himself by his claim that he followed the gods lead with a devotion to philosophy. He told his jury of 501 fellow male Athenians that he was a good person, and by understanding what to care about, he, therefore, knew how to behave. (Some scholars have suggested that Socrates was brought to trial because of his association with malfeasants during Athens defeat in the Peloponnesian War, and his silence during the oligarchs' reign of terror — 404 B.C. through 403 B.C. — had left him under suspicion.) The jury voted for conviction, and then (as it was the custom for Athenian criminal trials) the jury voted again for the penalty. After his indictment, Socrates proposed that he be fined thirty minas, and states that Plato, Crito, Critobulus and Aristobulus will guarantee the payment. "The jury now votes again and sentences Socrates to death."[21] Socrates tells the men of the jury, "Keep this truth in mind, that a good man cannot be harmed either in life or in death..."[22] On his last day in prison, his followers were with him, but absent from his deathbed was Plato, who said he was ill.[23] We can imagine that Plato lived forever in guilt because he was not there to serve the strength of his master at death's door. Lady philosophy did not abandon Socrates at his deathbed. Although absent in life, the esteemed thinker is present in spirit and beckons us to care for our souls. As we read Plato, we acknowledge a love for Socrates, but this bookish romance is not an acquaintance with that flesh-and-blood philosopher whose silveriness of eye was able to pierce the Athenian soul. Who should we trust in matters pertaining to the soul? The sea keeps that which is perfectly formed; their timbre is too brilliant for humankind's measure. In Socrates' physical absence, we are educated dryly; and so we learn which senses will favor a more fluid fulfillment, and through this difficult but spiritual task, we come — once again — upon his spirit.

CHAPTER THREE

The Divine Oracle: Jesus and Freedom

There is an ancient belief that the pagan oracles were all silenced with the birth of our Lord. Jesus of Nazareth was born approximately 4 B.C. (in the last years of the reign of King Herod the Great who died in 4 B.C.), (See Mat 2:1 and Luke 2:4-7) in Bethlehem in Judea. His father was Joseph, a carpenter, and His mother was Mary. The Bible tells us that Jesus' entry to this world was through virgin birth. "Now the birth of Jesus Christ was as follows: when His mother Mary had been betrothed to Joseph, before they came together she was found to be with child by the Holy Spirit" (Mat 1:18). Luke tells us that Jesus as a child was known to be precocious, and that He grew in strength and in wisdom, and that God's grace was upon Him (Luke 2:41-52). Jesus began his public ministry at the age of thirty (Luke 3:23). Jesus communicated via oral teaching (like Socrates), never placing pen to paper, and His language was Aramaic. He taught in the villages of lower Galilee and travelled to Jerusalem in the south, and possibly made some visits across Jordan, and travelled through Samaria on His way to Jerusalem. Some forty to seventy years after Jesus' lifetime, the Bible teaches us the Good Word. Like Socrates, we learn about Jesus' oral teachings through the writing of others: the Bible, especially the Gospels of Mathew, Mark, Luke and John, the Pauline Epistles, the first-century Jewish historian Josephus, and the Dead Sea Scrolls. We also gain an understanding of the world during the life of Jesus from the writings of Philo of Alexandria (an elder contemporary of Jesus), The Apostle Paul, Pliny the elder, and the Roman historian Tacitus.

An owl in the wilderness and an eagle of the sky — both Socrates and Jesus are historically described as temperate, modest, humble, and personable. Both men were physically strong and healthy, and showed restraint and fortitude in their actions, and each spoke of virtue; however, Socrates' thoughts regarding vice were gently voiced, while Jesus expressed a stronger indignation (for example, Mat 21:12-13; Luke 19:41-48; John 2:13-17). The Gospels describe the Savior's passionate cleansing of the temple mount where the moneychangers and animals were sold, although His ministry was nonviolent. Jesus instructed His disciples not to react aggressively and not to injure others. The philosopher and the Savior had strong personal friendships; we read about Socrates' personal attachments to his pupils and especially the handsome Alcibiades, and Jesus' friendship to Lazarus's family, His love for His apostles, His disciples, and His devotion and love for His mother, Mary. The religious, political and cultural climate of their eras provided the material for their teaching, and when we read about these men (one human and one divine), we are just as captivated today (as were the ancient citizens of their time) by their deep wisdom and open love for people in general, and their effective ability to teach their message.

We reflect upon the enlightenment of Socrates and Jesus' wisdom against the historical background of a superstitious ancient Athens and Rome. Under the protective wings of the owl and the eagle, we take refuge with the Sages of truth. "But when He, the Spirit of truth, comes, He will guide you into all the truth; for He will not speak on His own initiative, but whatever He hears, He will speak; and He will disclose to you what is to come" (John 16:13). We can imagine Jesus, as he fulfilled His divine mission on earth — he looked like an ordinary man whose hair was parted down the middle (a Nazarene custom of the time), large and wise eyes, a forked beard, and draped clothing of white linen that was a typical dress of the ancient Essenes. He worked as a carpenter so he had to have physical strength to work with stones as well as wood, with no hand tools. We read in the Bible how He could slip into crowds when it was necessary for Him to disappear (John 5:13, Luke 4:30, John 7:11, John 11:56). We also read about His spiritual magnetism that attracted crowds wherever He travelled, spoke the gospel, and performed miracles — as He gathered His twelve apostles and disciples around Him. Although Socrates did not perform any miracles, and he would not refer to his students as disciples, he did exhibit a personal magnetism that attracted crowds when he was teaching.

We come to the Christian table with a western philosophical heritage of ideas, concepts, and symbols, and although these concepts intersect in the secular realm, we learn to exercise our wings in the sacred province when we breach the spiritual domain. We are divinely guided in the spiritual realm and our intimacy with God is strengthened with the aid of divine symbols. As children of God, we study, for example, Moses and the pillars of fire guiding the Israelites, the Ark of the Holy Covenant, Noah's Ark, the Angelic Messengers of God, Jesus' Holy teaching, the Holy Cross, and the Holy Spirit. The symbolic truth leads us — systematically — to the absolute Truth of God; and, God's symbols remain sealed until we have the eyes to see, the intellect to understand, and the maturity to comprehend them. The Bible reveals meaning to us as we grow in our intimacy and love for God and His divine Son. The Apostle Paul spoke of these truths when he preached to the Jews about the Messiah, "But their minds were hardened; for until this very day at the reading of the old Covenant the same veil remains unlifted, because it is removed in Christ. But to this day whenever Moses is read, a veil lies over their heart; but whenever a person turns to the Lord, the veil is taken away" (2 Cor 3:14-16). Christianity teaches us that the Lord, by His Holy Spirit, will open our eyes, hearts and understanding of the Holy Words written in the Old and New Testaments.

The Four Gospels — Mathew, Mark, Luke and John — are harmonious books that shed light on our spiritual understanding as we read about the life and teaching of Jesus. The books of Mathew, Mark, Luke and John are collectively called the Gospels (*evaggelion*, Greek for 'good news'). All four Gospels tell us the story of Jesus' ministry, the gathering of His disciples, and His death and resurrection. Mathew, a tax collector and disciple of Christ, writes to show that Jesus was the long awaited King, the son of David, and the promised Messiah — by prophecy and fulfillment. Mathew (written between 52 and 68 A.D. - before the fall of Jerusalem) begins with a genealogy that shows Jesus as the heir and true king descended from the line of David. Mathew contains numerous Old Testament references to support the Biblical prophecy that Jesus was the anointed Son of Man. For example, Jesus quotes the prophecy of Isaiah as being fulfilled when He teaches, "But blessed are your eyes, because they see; and your ears because they hear" (Mat 13:16). In Mathew, Chapter 13, Jesus is teaching in parables (parabole), where the surface meaning of the parable introduces a profound mystery that require interpretation by the initiated. The disciples came to Jesus and asked Him why He speaks to the people in parables. He answered them, "To you it has been granted to know the mysteries of the kingdom of heaven, but to them it has not been granted" (Mat 13:11). In the story of the miraculous feeding of the crowd, the Gospels tell us that a large crowd had gathered in an isolated place near Bethsaida, across the northern end of the lake (Mat 14:13-21, Mark 6:32-44; Luke 9:10-17; and John 6:14-15). Some commentators have suggested that this was a deliberate gathering (since the people were outside the territory of

Herod Antipas) to force Jesus into a commitment for political action against their Roman oppressors. Mathew writes, "Seeing the people, He felt compassion for them, because they were distressed (*eskulmenoi* also translated as harassed) and dispirited (*errimmenoi* also translated as dejected) like sheep without a shepherd" (Mat 9:36). The Romans oppressed the people who were heavily taxed, living under indebtedness, and suffering from hard labor. This story of the miracle of the loaves demonstrates the miraculous power of Jesus, as well as His love and compassion toward others. The feeding of the people is also an analogy to the Old Testament story of manna in the desert (Ex 16), and Elisha's multiplication of loaves (2 Ki 4:42-44). Eating together was symbolic of unity and communion in the Kingdom of Heaven. This symbolic unity — found within sharing a meal — was also evident in ancient Athens where we find, for example, Socrates reclining at a banquet and teaching his fellow banqueters about the nature of love (see the *Symposium*). Jesus teaches, "Do not think that I came to abolish the Law or the Prophets; I did not come to abolish but to fulfill" (Mat 5:17). We understand from the gospel of Mathew that the Kingdom of God is a spiritual domain where the reign of God is possible through our submission to spiritual principles.

John Mark, who was a cousin of Barnabas and a companion to Peter, wrote the Gospel of Mark — written between 55 and 68 A.D. The Gospel of Mark teaches us that Jesus was the faithful servant of Jehovah, emphasizes His works, and edification of His teaching for Gentile Christians. Mark's Gospel writes about the humanity and imperfections of Jesus' twelve chosen disciples — even though Jesus gave them the power to drive out demons and heal sicknesses. Mark writes, "And He (Jesus) began to teach them that the Son of Man must suffer many things and be rejected by the elders and the chief priests and the scribes, and be killed, and after three days rise again" (Mark 8:31). Jesus stated this matter plainly when, "Peter took Jesus aside and began to rebuke Him" (Mark 8:32). Jesus responded, "Get behind Me, Satan; for you are not setting your mind on God's interests, but man's" (Mark 8:33). We are reminded of the Old Testament Psalm of David, "The Lord has sworn and will not change His mind, 'You are a priest forever According to the order of Melchizedek' " (Psalms 110:4). "On the first day of Unleavened Bread, when the Passover lamb was being sacrificed, His disciples said to Him, 'Where do You want us to go and prepare for You to eat the Passover?' " (Mark 14:12). (Jesus had already made arrangements.) "While they were eating, He took some bread, and after a blessing He broke it, and gave it to them, and said, 'Take it; this is My body' " (Mark 14:22). (Bread was the common Jewish food, and diluted wine, the common drink.) Jesus took a cup and gave thanks, and said, "This is My blood of the covenant, which is poured out for many...I will never drink of the fruit of the vine until that day when I drink it new in the kingdom of God" (Mark 14:24-25).

Luke, a physician and companion to the Apostle Paul, traveled with Paul to Jerusalem, accompanied him to Rome, continued with him in prison, and was with him until his death. (As well as the Gospel of Luke, he also wrote the book of Acts, written about 63 A.D.) Luke gives an historical account of Christianity to Theophilus, who is otherwise unknown. Luke begins his account with the time when Herod was king of Judea (Luke 1:5). At this time there was a priest named Zechariah — from the priestly division of Abijah — who was married to Elizabeth, a descendent of Aaron (Luke 1:5). Luke writes that Elizabeth was barren, and the couple were in advanced years (Luke 1:7). While Zechariah was performing his priestly duties of burning incense in the temple of the Lord, an angel of the Lord appeared before him and said, "your wife Elizabeth will bear you a son, and you will give him the name John" (Luke 1:13). Elizabeth was in her sixth month of pregnancy when the angel Gabriel was sent from God to a city in Galilee called Nazareth, "to a virgin engaged to a man whose name was Joseph, of the descendants of David; and the virgin's name was Mary" (Luke 1:26-27). The angel Gabriel said to Mary, "Greetings, favored one! The Lord is with you" (Luke 1:28). Luke tells us that Mary "was very perplexed at this statement...and salutation", (Luke 1:29), even though Gabriel was describing Mary as full of grace. The angel Gabriel said to Mary, "you will conceive in your womb and bear a son, and you shall name him Jesus. He will be great and will be called the Son of the Most High; and the Lord God will give Him the throne of His father David; and he will reign over the house of Jacob forever and His kingdom will have no end" (Luke 1:31-33). Mary asked how this could be possible when she was a virgin. (Luke 1:34) The angel answered her, "The Holy Spirit will come upon you, and the power of the Most High will over-shadow you; and for that reason the holy Child shall be called the Son of God" (Luke 1:35). Mary responded to the angelic message by going to stay with Elizabeth until just before the birth of her son (Luke 1:39-56). The birth of John the Baptist was the forerunner of the Lord as the voice calling in the desert, "make ready the way of the Lord" (Luke 3:4). John the Baptist's witness to Jesus marked the end of the old age of the law and the promise and the beginning of the new age of fulfillment (Luke 3:1-4). When John the Baptist baptized Jesus, the Holy Spirit came upon Him in order to equip Him for His work as the Messiah — Servant of the Lord. A heavenly voice confirmed the divine approval of Him as the Son of God — Jesus was empowered for the work that lay before Him.

After Jesus' baptism, the Holy Spirit led Him into the wilderness to prepare Him for His ministry. Luke writes, "Jesus full of the Holy Spirit, returned from the Jordan and was led around by the Spirit in the wilderness" (Luke 4:1). Jesus was in the desert for forty days and nights, and was hungry. Satan tempted Jesus to turn a stone into bread. Jesus answered the devil, "It is written, 'Man shall not live on bread alone' " (Luke 4:3-4). The devil offered Jesus the rule of the kingdoms of the imperial world — with all of the power and glory — if Jesus would worship him. Jesus answered him, "It is written, 'You shall worship the Lord your God and serve Him only.' " (Luke 4:8). Jesus demonstrated steadfast obedience to the will of His Father, and was not tempted by Satan's dark evil during his forty days in the wilderness. Luke writes, "When the devil had finished every temptation, he left Him until an opportune time" (Luke 4:13).

Jesus taught the Holy Word and He made a favorable impression on the people everywhere. His public ministry begins for Luke with the sermon in Nazareth, the town where Jesus grew up. Jesus teaches at Nazareth when He enters the Synagogue on the Sabbath (Luke 4:16). The book of the prophet Isaiah was handed to Him (Luke 4:17), and when the people wanted some visible proof of His claims that He is God's messianic herald of salvation, Jesus spoke against them and said, "No prophet is welcome in his hometown" (Luke 4:24). He told them that the gospel would ultimately go to the Gentiles. The people were enraged and they tried to throw Jesus down the cliff (Luke 4:28-29). "But passing through their midst, He went His way" (Luke 4:30).

Jesus' Galilean ministry is marked with the calling of His disciples and His teaching. Simon and his companions leave everything — families, work, boats, and friends — and follow Jesus (Luke 5:11). There were no "untouchables" in Jesus' ministry, and we see this when He heals a leper (Luke 5:12-13). Jesus heals a paralyzed man (Luke 5:17-26), and raises a widow's son who had died (Luke 7:15). Jesus showed how the new way of the kingdom of God contrasted with the Pharisaic emphasis on strict keeping of the law, and His actions and words angered them. Jesus teaches His disciples through dialogue (as Socrates taught his students), and through parables meant to convey spiritual concepts. Luke describes the Sermon on the Mount as the Sermon on the Plane, and Jesus teaches about the relationship of the disciples to God and to other people. Luke emphasizes the compassion of the Messiah. (We remember that although Socrates was not divine, he also demonstrated compassion toward others.)

Our loving and constant pursuit of God (*epektasis*) leads us to the sweetness of prayer. Our constant reaching forward and striving toward God (but never reaching His transcendence) is a notion from Apostle Paul when he says, "I press on so that I may lay hold of that for which also I was laid hold of by Christ Jesus" (Phil 3:12). "I press on toward the goal for the prize of the upward call of God in Christ Jesus" (Phil 3:14). Jesus' pious and obedient nature — who turns to God in prayer — is observed in the Gospels. We read in Luke, for example, how Jesus healed the man whose right hand was withered. The Scribes and Pharisees were filled with rage because He healed on the Sabbath and they discussed what they might do to Jesus. "It was at this time that He went off to the mountain to pray, and He spent the whole night in prayer to God" (Luke 6:12). When the day came, "He called His disciples to Him and chose twelve of them, whom He also names as apostles" (Luke 6:13).

In Luke, prayer is linked with significant spiritual events where there is a manifestation of God's power. Jesus took three of His disciples (Peter, John, and James), up to the mountain to pray with Him. "Now Peter and his companions had been overcome with sleep; but when they were fully awake, they saw His glory and the two men standing with Him" (Luke 9:32). In the transfiguration, Jesus was praying and in contact with the heavenly world when He was transfigured — His appearance and garments took on a heavenly light.

Moses and Elijah, who represented, respectively, the law and the prophets, joined Him. God's presence was indicated by a cloud and the heavenly voice, "This is My Son, *My* Chosen One; listen to Him!" (Luke 9:35). Compare what had been said at the baptism of Jesus, "You are My beloved Son, in You I am well-pleased" (Luke 3:22). There are three accounts of the transfiguration of Jesus in the gospels: Mathew, Mark, and Luke. This author has always been perplexed why John did not record the events in his Gospel (none of the three witnesses to the transfiguration, Peter, John, and James gave personal accounts, but we find three versions in the Gospels of Mathew, Mark, and Luke). This mystical experience that illuminated Jesus, Moses and Elijah in a radiant and spiritual splendor would leave the disciples with a deep and profound belief in Jesus' divinity and God's power and supremacy.

Jesus taught the disciples to proclaim that the kingdom of God had arrived, and the signs of its presence were the mighty works that they would perform. They were to live simply, and could accept hospitality but were not to seek for better accommodations. Jesus further taught the disciples that they must be ready to place God's commands above family and self, and be ready for martyrdom or to die to all personal desires. The kingdom of God is for those who are prepared to receive it like a little child in a humble and receptive frame of mind. Jesus taught through parables: the rich fool (Luke 12:13-21), the mustard seed and the yeast (Luke 13:18-

21), the narrow door (Luke 13:24), the great banquet (Luke 14:15-24), the cost of being a disciple (Luke 14:25-35), the lost sheep (Luke 15:1-7), the lost coin (Luke 15:8-10), the lost son (Luke 15:11-31), the shrewd manager (Luke 16:1-15), the persistent widow (Luke 18:1-8), and the ten minas (Luke 19:11-26). These parables are an example of teaching inductively — we see examples of all the particular things, and these particulars point to the universal idea or concept within the parable.

Luke writes about the Last Supper and the treachery of Judas' plan to betray Jesus (Luke 22:1-6). Jesus was arrested in the garden of Gethsemane (Luke 22:39-54, Mat 26:36-46), and was brought before Pilate, who tried to avoid settling a difficult case, so he sent Jesus to Herod Antipas, who — in turn — set him back to Pilate, who sentenced Jesus to death, and punished Him by scourging — a cruel whipping prior to the crucifixion. After being crucified between two criminals, Jesus' first recorded words in Luke were a prayer for forgiveness for His executioners. Darkness fell over the land, "and the veil of the temple was torn in two" (Luke 23:45). Jesus cried out in a loud voice, " 'Father into your Hands I commit my Spirit.' Having said this, He breathed His last" (Luke 23:46).

Joseph of Arimathea (The Bible tells us he was from a city of the Jews) asked Pilate for the body of Jesus, took the body down, wrapped Him in a linen cloth and laid Him in a tomb cut into the rock (Luke 23:50-53). "The women who had come with Him out of Galilee followed and saw the tomb and how His body was laid," writes Luke (Luke 23:55). "And on the Sabbath they rested according to the commandment" (Luke 23:56). When the women returned the next day to the tomb bringing spices, which they had prepared for the body, they found the stone rolled away from the tomb (Luke 24:1-3). Two men suddenly stood near them in dazzling clothing and said, "He is not here, but He has risen. Remember how he spoke to you...,saying that the Son of man must be delivered into the hands of sinful men, and be crucified, and the third day rise again" (Luke 24:6-7). Luke provides three accounts of Jesus' resurrection appearances: the women at the tomb (Luke 24:1-10), the appearance to two disciples on the road to Emmaus (Luke 24:13-35), and the appearance to the eleven disciples in Jerusalem (Luke 24:36-51). Jesus appeared to His disciples, they ate with Him, they touched His flesh, and He taught them, "These are My words which I spoke to you while I was still with you, that all things which are written about Me in the Law of Moses and the Prophets and the Psalms must be fulfilled" (Luke 24:44). Luke concludes his Gospel with a short account of Jesus' ascension to heaven after speaking with His disciples (Luke 24:51). Luke's account of Jesus is a story of the perfect Son of Man, the Anointed Preacher, and the Savior of lost humanity. Luke shows the Greeks that Jesus was the only Savior — the Messiah from the lineage of King David. Luke's Gospel presents the factual aspects of the Lord's life, humanity, and ministry.

The Gospel of John (traditionally attributed to the Apostle John) presents the inner spiritual aspects of the Lord's life, including His doctrine, discourses, and Judean ministry from Capernaum to Jerusalem. John's gospel demonstrates to us how God teaches us through symbols, discourses, and dialectic. (Remember that the ancient philosopher Socrates also used symbols, discourses, and dialectic to teach.) John uses vivid and striking language to generate symbolic opposites, for example, lightness, and darkness. John's portrayal of Jesus is the Word (*logos*) made flesh, and He engages His disciples in long discourses and theological questions, for example, knowledge and belief, and eternal life. Jesus as Son of God is prominent in the Gospel of John. We study this Gospel by utilizing an inductive methodology, for example, the Son of God terminology harkens back to the Old Testament prophecy. The Gospel of John begins with the inspirational words, "In the beginning was the Word, and the Word was with God, and the Word was God. He was in the beginning with God" (John 1:1-2). We are given much to think about: the Word's eternal preexistence, and involvement in creation (John 1:1-5), John as a witness to the Light (John 1:6-8), and the worlds rejection of the Light (John 1:10). The Apostle John writes, "No one has seen God at any time; the only begotten God who is in the bosom of the Father, He has explained Him" (John 1:18). We learn more about Jesus gathering His disciples: Andrew and Peter follow Jesus (John 1:35-42), Simon called Cephas, which means "rock" and was translated Peter (John 1:42), then Philip and Nathanael follow Christ (John 1:43-51).

Jesus performed many miracles during His short and glorious ministry on earth. Unlike Socrates — who did not perform any miracles, but did profess to his *daimonia* (his spiritual voice that guided him in actions not to take), Jesus' heritage as Son of God was manifested in the actions that He took. Jesus changed water into wine, healed the sick, raised the dead, calmed stormy seas, walked on the sea, was not guilty of any sins, and He was resurrected. Jesus, for example, attends the wedding at Cana of Galilee with His mother and His disciples. When the wine runs out, Jesus turns water into wine — the beginning of His signs which manifested His glory, "and His disciples believed in Him" (John 2:3-11). Jesus has a conversation with Nicodemus (a high-ranking Jewish rabbi), "God did not send His Son into the world to judge the world, but that the world might be saved through Him" (John 3:17).

During this ancient time, it was inappropriate for a Rabbi to speak with a woman; Jesus broke this prejudice, and His disciples did not question Him. As an example, He came upon a Samaritan woman at the well as He passed through Samaria on His way to Galilee. The Samaritan woman said, "I know that the Messiah is coming (He who is called Christ); when that One comes, He will declare all things to us" (John 4:25). Jesus replied, "I who speak to you am He" (John 4:26). This is an important Biblical passage because for the first time, Jesus is stating that He is the Messiah! The Samaritan woman went into the town to tell the townspeople about Jesus (John 4:28-29). Meanwhile the disciples urged Jesus to eat, and He said, "I have food to eat that you do not know about" (John 4:32). "My food is to do the will of Him who sent Me and to accomplish His work" (John 4:34). Many of the Samaritans believed in Jesus because of the woman's testimony (John 4:39-42). The Bible teaches us that Jesus performed the miracles of His divine mission through the direction of God.

Jesus leaves Judea and goes into Galilee, and performs his second miracle in Canaan where he heals the Royal official's son at Capernaum (John 4:46-54). Then He heals the lame man at the pool of Bethesda (John 5:1-15). It was the Sabbath on that day and the Jews said to the man who was healed at the pool of Bethesda, "It is the Sabbath, and it is not permissible for you to carry your pallet" (John 5:10). The Jews were seeking to kill Jesus because, "He not only was breaking the Sabbath, but also was calling God His own Father, making Himself equal with God" (John 5:18). He answered them by saying, "The Son can do nothing of Himself, unless it is something He sees the Father doing; for whatever the Father does, these things the Son also does in like manner" (John 5:19).

Then Jesus went to the other side of the Sea of Galilee (or Tiberias), and a large crowd followed Him because they saw the miracles of healing on the sick (John 6:1-2). "Then Jesus went up on the mountain, and there He sat down with His disciples" (John 6:3). A large crowd gathered and Jesus had compassion on them and healed their sick (Mat 14:14). The disciples said to Jesus, "This place is desolate and the hour is already late; so send the crowds away, that they may go into the villages and buy food for themselves" (Mat 14:15). We learn from the Gospels that Jesus had compassion on the multitude for they had nothing to eat, and performs the miracle of feeding five-thousand people from five small barley loaves and two small fish. The people said, "This is truly the Prophet who is to come into the world" (John 6:14). He perceives that the people want to take Him by force and make Him King, so he withdraws to the mountain by Himself (John 6:15). The disciples started in a boat across the sea to Capernaum when a strong wind stirred up the sea. Then they saw Him walking on the stormy sea toward the boat, and He tells them not to be afraid (John 6:20). Jesus then teaches them about the bread of life, "I am the living bread that came down out of heaven; if anyone eats of this bread, he will live forever; and the bread also which I will give for the life of the world is My flesh" (John 6:51). Jesus' teaching of the bread of life (which was not understood by the disciples) caused many of his followers to desert Him (John 6:60-72).

Jesus goes to the temple in the midst of the Feast of Booths to teach (John 7:14). The chief priests and the Pharisees sent temple guards to arrest Him (John 7:32). Jesus goes to the Mount of Olives, and then in the morning went to the temple again to teach, "I go away, and you will seek Me, and will die in your sin; where I am going, you cannot come" (John 8:21). "I do nothing on my own initiative, but I speak these things as the Father taught me" (John 8:28). "And you will know the truth, and the truth will make you free" (John 8:32). Jesus said to them, "Truly, truly, I say to you, before Abraham was born, I am" (John 8:58). The crowd then "picked up stones to throw at Him, but Jesus hid Himself and went out of the temple" (John 8:59).

Jesus heals a man born blind on the Sabbath and the Pharisees said, "This man is not from God, because

He does not keep the Sabbath" (John 9:16). Jesus teaches, "While I am in the world, I am the Light of the world" (John 9:5). The Pharisees interrogate the formerly blind man (John 9:13-17), and his parents (John 9:18-23), and Jesus teaches the Pharisees about their spiritual blindness. In a lovely analogy of the shepherd and his flock Jesus states, "I am the good shepherd, and I know My own and My own know Me," (John 10:14). Jesus said to them, "the Father knows me and I know the Father" (John 10:15). Lazarus had been dead for four days when Jesus raised him from the dead (John 11:39-44). The chief priests and the Pharisees sought to kill Jesus because of the signs that he performed (John 11:47-53). Six days before Passover a dinner was given in honor of Jesus, "Martha was serving; but Lazarus was one of those reclining at the table with Him" (John 12:1-2). "Mary then took a pound of very costly perfume of pure nard, and anointed the feet of Jesus and wiped His feet with her hair; and the house was filled with the fragrance of the perfume" (John 12:3). On Palm Sunday Jesus made a triumphal entry into Jerusalem riding on a donkey. These things were written in the Bible — "Fear not, Daughter of Zion; behold, your King is coming, seated on a donkey's colt" (John 12:15). A large crowd went out to meet Him and the people took palm branches and began to shout, "Hosanna! Blessed is He who comes in the name of the Lord, even the King of Israel" (John 12:13). Jesus predicts His death, "Now My soul has become troubled and what shall I say, 'Father save Me from this hour'? But for this purpose I came to this hour' " (John 12:27). "Father glorify your name, Then a voice came out of heaven: 'I have both glorified it, and will glorify it again'" (John 12:28).

While the Jews were hardening their hearts toward Jesus, He turns His attention to His beloved disciples. The evening meal was served when Jesus took off His outer clothing, wrapped a towel around His waist, and in an act of humble love and caring, poured water into a basin and began to wash His disciples' feet (John 13:5). "If I then the Lord and Teacher washed your feet, you also ought to wash one another's feet" (John 13:14). In the Gospel of John, His disciples and others regularly address Jesus as Teacher and Lord. Jesus prophetically states, "Truly, truly, I say to you, that one of you will betray me" (John 13:21). John was lovingly leaning on Jesus' bosom and asked, "Lord, who is it?" (John 13:25). Satan entered into Judas and Jesus said to Judas, "What you do, do quickly" (John 13:27). "Little children, I am with you a little while longer you will seek me...where I am going, you cannot come" (John 13:33). Jesus then predicts Peter's denial, "A rooster will not crow until you deny Me three times" (John 13:38). "I am the way, and the truth, and the life; no one comes to the Father but through Me" (John 14:6). "Do you not believe that I am in the Father, and the Father is in Me? The words that I say to you I do not speak on My own initiative, but the Father abiding in Me does His works" (John 14:10). The Savior teaches them, "If you love Me, you will keep My commandments." (John 14:15). "I will ask the Father, and He will give you another Helper, that He may be with you forever; I will not leave you as orphans; I will come to you. After a little while the world will no longer see Me, but you will see Me; because I live, you will live also" (John 14:16-19). "The Helper, the Holy Spirit, whom the Father will send in My name, He will teach you all things, and bring to your remembrance all that I said to you" (John 14:26). "Peace I leave with you" (John 14:27).

Jesus goes to Kidron Valley (to the garden of Gethsemane) with His disciples in order to pray (John 18:1). Judas betrayed Him, and led the Romans, the chief priests, and the Pharisees there — with lanterns, torches, and weapons (John 18:3). Simon Peter — defending Jesus — cuts off the right ear of the high priest's slave, and Jesus said to him, "Put the sword into the sheath; the cup which the Father has given Me, shall I not drink it?" (John 18:11). They arrested and bound Him, and took Him, first, to the High Priest Annas (father-in-law of Caiaphas) (John 18:12-13). "Caiaphas had advised the Jews that it was expedient for one man to die on behalf of the people" (John 18:14). Annas questioned Jesus then sent Him — bound — to Caiaphas (John 18:24). As predicted by Jesus, Peter denied knowing Him (John 18:27). Then Jesus was led to the Praetorium where Pilate asked Him, "Are you the King of the Jews" (John 18:33). Jesus answered, "You say correctly that I am a king. For this I have been born, and for this I have come into the world, to testify to the truth. Everyone who is of the truth hears My voice" (John 18:37). Pilate said, "I find no guilt in Him" (John 18:38). It was a custom for the Romans to release someone at the Passover, and so Pilate asked the Jews if they wanted to release the King of the Jews. They cried out, "Not this Man, but Barabbas (who was a robber)" (John 39-40). Pilate sentenced Jesus to death, and punished Jesus by scourging — a cruel whipping prior to the crucifixion (John 19:1). "And the soldiers twisted together a crown of thorns and put it on His head, and put a purple robe on Him; and they began to come up to him and say, 'Hail, King of the Jews' and to give Him slaps in the face" (John 19:2-3).

They crucified Jesus on Golgotha, and the soldiers divided lots so that they could take His clothing. Standing by the cross was His beloved mother, Mary, and the disciple, John, whom He loved was nearby, when Jesus said to His mother, "Behold your son," and He said to His disciple John, "Behold your mother" (John 19:26-27). Joseph of Arimathea, a secret disciple for fear of reprisal from the Jews, asked Pilate for the body of Jesus (John 19:38). He took the body to "a new tomb in which no one had yet been laid" (John 19:41).

When Mary Magdalene came early to the tomb on the first day of the week, she found the stone rolled away from the tomb (John 20:1). Mary ran to get Simon Peter and John, and said to them, "They have taken away the Lord out of the tomb, and we do not know where they have laid Him" (John 20:2). The two disciples ran to the tomb and Simon Peter entered, and "he saw and believed" (John 20:4, 8). "For as yet they did not understand the Scripture, that He must rise again from the dead" (John 20:9). Mary was standing outside the tomb and weeping, and two angels in white were sitting, one at the head, and one at the feet, where the body of Jesus had been lying (John 20:12). "Remember how he spoke to you and said that the Son of man must be delivered into the hands of sinful men, and be crucified, and the third day rise again" (Luke 24:7). Mary turned and saw Jesus standing there, but she did not recognize Him. He asked her why she was weeping. (John 20:15) Jesus said to her, "Mary!" Mary turned to Him and said in Hebrew "Rabboni!" (which means, Teacher) (John 20:16). John concludes his gospel with Jesus commanding His beloved disciples to, "Come and have breakfast" (John 21:12). This was the third time that Jesus manifested Himself to the disciples after His resurrection (John 21:14). Jesus instructs His disciples to "Tend My sheep" (John 21:17). The gospel of John leaves us with the profound and holy teaching that Jesus did not leave us as orphans, but left the power of the Holy Spirit to teach and guide us.

CHAPTER FOUR

"Know Thyself": Socratic Wisdom

The historical heart beats in remembrance, not imbued with Pythagorean superstition, i.e., to initiate one into unending panaceas, but for an advancement in philosophy and religion. Let us remember that Socrates refused initiation — for philosophers will make no covenant with the Young Queen; the prodigious gambit in history is fortified not by the Red Lion, but by the Nemean, whose herculean strength is matched within the inextricable discipline of ratiocination. Let us be spectators in attendance at the extraordinary masquerade of the past, but to unmask only that which has camouflaged the eye of the intellect — for no spectacular mummery may disguise an accomplished actor in those things in which we take no part.

Our search for knowledge and a deeper meaning to life is a very human desire found in other ancient philosophic and religious disciplines. Siddharta Gautama was born in Lumbini, Nepal, and died approximately 400 B.C., and his meditation under the Bodhi tree led to his enlightenment. He created the Buddhist Middle Way where we seek a moderate path between extreme behaviors, for example, between self-indulgence and asceticism. The philosopher Confucius (551-479 B.C.) founded Confucianism as a search for a way of life using a set of moral and political doctrines. Confucius taught personal and political morality, social and governmental relationships, justice, sincerity, virtue, cultivation of knowledge, and respect for family and elders. His teachings were compiled in the *Analects*. An example of his aphorisms is an early version of what we call the Golden Rule, (often referred to as the "Silver Rule"): "What you do not wish for yourself, do not do to others." Socrates was ten years old when Confucius passed away. Hebraic monotheism appeared during the days of the Hebrew prophets in the 8th century B.C. At the time of Socrates, the Jewish tribes descended from Abraham were worshipping the one God Yahweh, whose ineffable holiness, purity and transcendence remains a mystery, but at the same time, Yahweh intervenes and is engaged in human concerns.

As philosophers, we are lovers of truth, but not just any truth — like Socrates, we seek knowledge of the nature of the beautiful itself — for Christians the beautiful is the light that emanates from God. God is light and love! In the *Republic*, Plato distinguishes between opinion and knowledge: we naturally have opinions for we are lovers of beautiful sights, sounds, and colors; however, we do not have knowledge of the beautiful thing itself. We gain this insight by way of knowledge of the particulars (via induction) — as our minds climb the ladder of understanding from the details to the universal. For Plato, knowledge is knowledge of the beautiful in itself.[24] We seek out Socrates for wisdom and for ideas that will lead us on our upward spiritual journey. He was extraordinary in the peculiar attraction and influence that he exerted over those who encountered him; and it is this magnetism, which draws us in our search for the clarity of spiritual concepts. We take a special seat beside Socrates as we learn to develop and utilize these spiritual ideas; however, our efforts are not complete until we ascertain how these apply to us. The philosopher not only seeks the desire to live a long life, but pursues a quality of life as well. This quality of existence flows out of our desires, and our yearnings in turn, are stimulated by these notions. We discover the inadequacy of some of our concepts when we test them against the material of our everyday life, thus becoming aware of what deserves to be desired.

The salt of Socrates' wisdom is found in the value that it gives to us as individuals who seek freedom. Our heritage as Americans is one of "seekers of ideas"; we have a traditional lineage in the "concepts of freedom". We acknowledge and use sound concepts that in turn stimulate impressions and open our intellect for the meeting of minds in the physical environment — like Socrates and his students. The sensitivity of humankind for intellectual dynamism is demonstrated throughout the ideational history, not just in the United States but elsewhere in the world. The whole corpus of ideas refers us back to our humanity and an examination of our knowledge for a determination of that which is worthy of being known. There is no more critical time for this examination than now in the computer age, where we have such vast quantities of information — accessible and readily available. We know that not all information is valuable to us, and so the key is to progress Socratically (dialectically with question and answer) with an examination of some of the important questions of our age. The ancient Socratic quest to progress from that which seems to be to that which is known gives us a clue in tracking sound theories; any obscurity can be a double indemnity against our understanding due to the ideational prejudices that encumber us. To comprehend how we ought to penetrate the historical concepts and break through these prejudices, let us undergo a metamorphosis back to 399 B.C. when Socrates was accused of impiety and worshiping strange gods, and corrupting the youth of Athens. There has been so much written about Socrates throughout the years that many accounts have rendered him to be a myth-like character of god-like proportions. We can use our own historical imagination where we envision the Athenian court where they condemn him to death. Criton, Socrates' lifelong friend, visits him in prison, and tries to persuade him to escape to Thessaly; however, Socrates informs Criton that it is never right to do an injustice, or to defend offensive behavior when confronted with evil.

If Socrates had listened to Criton and disregarded the court's judgment, we would have witnessed an action that would have been incompatible with Socrates' belief in justice. Let us be spectators at this historical travesty, however, let us not linger at his deathbed, but be witness to his teachings and come away enlightened and refreshed — as Socrates himself would want us to be.

We ask ourselves, truly now, do we really live by our ideas and beliefs? We decipher our personal beliefs through awareness of our limitations and possible paths that are open to us, and the logical outcome of our actions. Our compatible possibilities are paired within a doxastic scope, for when an individual is immovable relative to a conviction, then the consequences of that belief will pervade all subsequent ideas and actions. Socrates would tell us that we must be vigilant in diagnosing what we embrace and what we negate. An enlightened understanding of beliefs — that Socrates taught — holds that our ideas are experimental and dialectical, and if our ideas clash with our beliefs, then we must reexamine those positions. Today, the contemplation of novel ideas can lead us into a paralyzing mental state, where we are under the impression that if we think it, it must exist. We sanctify our ideas, for they should be considered the heart of life in our human and spiritual development, not the death of the intellect in infinite abstractions. To live is to be able to think; and to think is to be able to exercise our ideas and spiritual gifts as human beings who are seeking for the best behavior guided by our tenets.

In picking up that golden thread of knowledge in Athens, and weaving the ancient meanings into modernity, we are not trying to recreate an Attic community, but to reacquaint ourselves with those ideas that can assist us in the activities of rational, spiritual and free human beings. For Socrates, an unexamined life is not worth living, "it is impossible for me to keep quiet because that means disobeying the god."[25] He needed to examine himself as well as other Athenians, for he felt that this was his divine mission! A virtuous person — like Socrates — always aims at actions that will improve others, and will never harm people. Socrates' vocation aimed at teaching people how to care for their souls, and to share his knowledge of truth, perfection, and wisdom. "Good Sir, you are an Athenian, a citizen of the greatest city with the greatest reputation for both wisdom and power; are you not ashamed of your eagerness to possess as much wealth, reputation and honors as possible, while you do not care for nor give thought to wisdom or truth, or the best possible state of your soul?"[26] Each soul must possess its own virtue and the soul's function is to manage and rule over itself; an ordered soul has a goal of virtuous action. The voice of Socrates admonishes us to maintain intellectual humility throughout our critical examination. All philosophers seek knowledge; but we are cautioned by Socrates to know virtue first, for upon our hunt for goodness, we become acquainted with the function of our human life and its meaning and purpose. All virtues are different applications of the knowledge of good and evil, i.e., he who knows what is right will then act according to his ethics. In our passion for understanding these values in order to live as good human beings, and to develop a good city, we will use our intellect, reason, soul, and our heart. Our development of a good city requires reason and a spiritual life, but we must remember that reason is not our god, but one tool for developing that, which is good, and this tool will lead us to a true heart — worship of God. Therefore, it is our goal to witness the passing of night's scepter to day's crown in persuading Athenian wisdom and philosophic stateliness to live amongst us as we develop as spiritual beings within our modern city — today.

We keep an open mind and heart as we discover the Socratic virtues; this philosophy has shackled us forever, willingly, to him, the one person to whom no draught of hemlock could ever vanquish. Can we appeal to the primal stream to cast up Socrates for instruction in the ancient wisdom of that which is good and beautiful, and through this education set forth, like Socrates, as virtuous citizens? A much used and proper allocation for wisdom is, 'Socrates is wise'; but what is really meant when we attribute the characteristic of 'being wise' to someone — as if wisdom overpowers one unknowingly out of an excess of knowledge. Socrates would be the first one to say that his wisdom came from knowing that he knew nothing. He lived during a period of time when there were many charlatans and magicians who claimed that they had unique powers, and he was not pleased that the Sophists taught how to win an argument for financial gain. Protagorist (for instance) charged high fees and taught young men from rich or noble families, how to "get ahead" in life. We follow seekers of wisdom — for we are all laborers here — those beings who emulate sound ideas, and in doing so they stimulate others in productive mental habits, for a wise person will willingly share their knowledge for the nourishment and development (intellectual, spiritual, physical, and material) of others. Moreover, this solid platform will provide a latitude of freedom for the functions of material and spiritual tasks. Philosophers are concerned with the best of possible worlds, i.e., the spiritual, moral, political, economic, and social order most conducive for practicing philosophy; and those laws, which follow from the definition of the thing in question, illuminate these regions. Existence conjoined with axiological ideas is a union-in-action of the existential and free for the human being. Already in possession of the riches of humankind, we become free when administered to by those individuals whose spirit is dilated by ideas, and this care is distributed within the philosopher's breadth of pace, i.e., in the self-knowledge that he knows not, but remains steady, resolved, and responsive to the circumstances of the occasion.

CHAPTER FIVE

The Inspiration for Inductive Methodology

No mind has so profoundly used induction for our guidance than Socrates — through the pen of Plato. Socrates used induction in ancient Greece to teach his fellow Athenians philosophy. To observe well is to interpret well — interpretation is defined as the art of explaining or telling the meaning of something and presenting it in understandable terms. The Platonic skills of Socrates can assist us in sharpening our tools for hermeneutics — the science and art of interpretation. On the mundane level, we learn Socratic dialectic and employ inductive reasoning in our studies. However, dialectic is more than the art of forming concepts and the art of question and answer, for it denotes checking the stream of thought at every step until you secure the understanding of an intelligent interlocutor. During the process, we note all of the relevant distinctions, similarities, agreements, contrasts, divisions, and ambiguities in ideas, concepts, and terms. Dialectic is a critical methodology that opens the intellectual horizons for a wider inquiry into the nature of things. Our goal is to search for correct concepts, whereby everything (the particulars) will radiate from its general conception, and then we can judge the truth of things. We seek out symbols and learn from them: from the Platonic Cave to Socrates' meaning of that which is Good and the Socratic *daimonion* (or spiritual guide or voice that guided Socrates in what actions to avoid) which teaches us that our knowledge increases with the aid of these symbols. For example, in the Platonic Cave analogy, the symbolic truth leads us, step by step, to the absolute truth of the Platonic Good.

Logos is an important term used in philosophy, religion, psychology, and rhetoric. Originally, it was a word meaning "a ground", "a plea", "an opinion", "word", "speech", or "reason": for example, both Plato and Aristotle used the term *logos* along with *rhema* to refer to sentences and propositions. Some modern Christian theologians use the term *logos* to refer to the written scriptures, and the term *rhema* to refer to the revelation received by the reader from the Holy Spirit when the Word *(Logos)* is read. The ancient Greek philosophers established patterns of thinking (Socrates 469-399 B.C., Plato 428/7-348/7 B.C., and Aristotle 384-322 B.C.) where questions were asked about the nature of things. Plato's pattern of thinking looked beyond particulars in the immediate world to the universal or the ultimate things that were real. We can benefit from the intellectual tools provided to us by these philosophers, that is, inductive reasoning, dialectic, and the understanding of symbols, concepts, and ideas to enlarge our minds with the principles of logic, knowledge, understanding, and communication.

Inductive methodology can provide us with the tools to reason, persuade, think, teach, learn, obtain premises, question, answer, come to have beliefs, and study. Socrates practiced inductive reasoning when he questioned others in search of a cognitive process — stepping from particulars to universals. Socrates' contribution in philosophy was vast as he led the quest for clarity, definitions, and reasoning. He sought definitions for terms like justice, virtue, the Good, the Beautiful, love and piety. He taught us that unless we could define these terms, then one would not know the true meaning. He practiced inductive reasoning whenever he sought universal definitions; for example, he inquired whether virtue could be taught, and in order to know this, the term "virtue" must first be defined.[27] Therefore, he set out on a dialectic quest — questioning others to discover what particulars were held in common. Meno responds to Socrates' stating that virtue is different for men, women (free or slaves), and children. Socrates politely argues that there must be some virtue common to all human beings, and asserts; "This generous action is virtuous", thereby you could draw the conclusion (via induction) that, "All generous actions are thereby virtuous". For Socrates, all definitions of a term would provide an objective basis to begin the search for knowledge. All opinion must stand the test of critical inspection, and Socrates was a master in cross-examination (*elenchus*) discovering what the interlocutor knew and did not know. He prompted everyone — both young and old, shoemakers, blacksmiths, politicians, playwrights, and citizens of every stratum — to ponder this and critically examine their knowledge of terms.

We are analyzing creatures, and inductive and deductive reasoning is part of our organizing mind-set. As spiritual beings, our goal for this logic is a clearer vision of God and His purposes for us. We utilize the logical tools that the ancient Greeks bequeathed to us, but we do not worship a multitude of gods — powerful and in need of assuagement — that sent the Athenians to the altars daily to fulfill their rites and rituals. The ancients' prayers appeased the gods so that the divinities would grant favor to Athena's children. Even the enlightened golden age of the Greeks was resplendent with temples and centers of worship for sacrifices in order to grant the gods' favor on the populace. Socrates was not superstitious in an age of superstition, chicanery, and magic, but he humbly made the necessary sacrifices that were required of an Athenian who wished to remain a model citizen. Throughout Plato's *Dialogues,* we hear Socrates offering a prayer to the gods, "O dear Pan and all the other gods of this place, grant that I may be beautiful inside. Let all my external possessions be in friendly harmony with what is within. May I consider the wise man rich. As for gold, let me have as much as a moderate man could bear and carry with him."[28] Although Socrates was born in an age of superstition, he rode the crest of reason above the Dionysian and Orphic cults. Socrates battled dead philosophy and in doing so, he gave us a moral compass for our individual actions.

We do not have the religious consciousness of the ancient Greeks, but we marvel at their veneration of Athena — the goddess of wisdom, learning, strategy in war, courage, inspiration, law, justice, and mathematics. Athena was the daughter of Zeus — king of the gods whose sphere was the sky, weather, hospitality, the rights of guests, sender of omens, punisher of injustice, and governor of the universe — and his first wife Metis. Athena's name denotes wisdom symbolized by the owl — a form that mythology reports that she often took. Metis warned Zeus that their son would be more powerful than Zeus himself. Upset, Zeus swallowed Metis, who was pregnant with their child, and this swallowing gave Zeus a headache, so he split his head open with an axe and out of his head came a fully-grown Athena dressed in her armor and helmet. Plato gives the etymology of Athena's name, "That is a grave matter, and there, my friend, the modern interpreters of Homer may, I think, assist in explaining the view of the ancients. For most of these in their explanations of the poet, assert that he meant by Athena "mind" (*nous*) and "intelligence" (*dianoia*), and the maker of names appears to have had a singular notion about her, and indeed calls her by a still higher title, "divine intelligence" (*theou noesis*), as though he would say: This is she who has the mind of God (*a theonoa*)."[29] Athena's most famous temple, the Parthenon on the Acropolis is where the queenly patron of the golden city commanded a view of her metropolis. The master sculptor Phidias created the statue *Athena Promachos* (mid-

5th century B.C.) — as she stood on the Acropolis, armored in virtue, her bronze helmet and spear tip gleamed in the sunlight, and was visible by sailors traveling to her glorious city. The Temple of Athena Nike — built in her honor during the 5th century B.C. — was constructed at the southwest corner of the Acropolis bastion, to the right of the Propylaea (gateway). Inside the Temple was a wingless wooden statue of Athena holding a pomegranate and helmet — a token of abundance and war. Plato writes about Athena's wisdom, "This is in fact nothing less than the very same system of social order that the goddess first devised for you when she founded your city, which she did once she had chosen the region in which your people were born, and had discerned that the temperate climate in it throughout the seasons would bring forth men of surpassing wisdom."[30]

The same fertile soil that grew the sacred olive trees (gifted to Athens by Athena), also gave birth to the age of philosophy. The ancient Pre-Socratics were fond of looking into the essences of things and we see this trend in Thales of Miletus, who proposed, "water was the elemental thing that never changed". Anaximander the Milesian proposed that the universal substance that was indeterminate and without specific qualities was air. Heraclitus of Ephesus claimed that at the heart of the universe was fire — fire was always in flux (*panta rhei*), and change was the only reality. Disagreeing with Heraclitus, Parmenides taught that immutable permanence was what was essential in the universe. Empedocles of Acragas in Sicily proposed that there were four basic elements, out of which everything else was composed: earth, air, fire, and water.

Democritus taught that atoms *(a-toma)* — indivisible particles too small for us to see — were combined in different arrangements to form the compounds in the universe. These philosophers all had a common assumption, i.e., that the experienced phenomena is not reality, and so they searched for that ultimate, eternal and unchanging essence, and then taught others how to perceive this reality. Pythagoras, (like Socrates who wrote nothing down), was believed to possess magical powers. He taught *metempsychosis* (reincarnation), the doctrine of the immortality of the soul, found deep mystical and philosophical significance in numbers, and discovered the Pythagorean Theorem.

Pythagoras influenced Plato's thinking and we can speculate if these great philosophers could hear the harmonic chords whose musical intervals created the Music of the Spheres, and indeed, we are told by the ancients, that the sage Pythagoras perceived this celestial music!

From the pre-Socratic philosophers we move to Plato, who writes creatively and imaginatively in prose with dialogues, where we can readily imagine the human characters interacting with one another in a discussion of Socratic dialectic. We learn philosophy (still applicable today) and ancient Athenian religion from Plato's engaging prose style. For example, unlike the omnipotence of the Christian God, the ancient Greeks imposed limitations on divine power. We learn that Socrates did not believe that the gods were the cause of evil things, but were harbingers of good things. Socrates taught that we err when the material body is greedy for pleasure and the satisfaction of material objects. The soul is the intellectual and moral aspect of the person, and can recognize and understand virtue, and apply this knowledge to personal understanding and to the polis. Socrates rigorously examined others in his quest for knowledge, the nature of virtue, and wisdom. He believed that it was only when you seek the goodness in others are you able to find that goodness in yourself. He stimulated his followers to think for themselves, to ask questions, to examine and reexamine concepts, and to search within for the truth to the answer. Socratic queries had the powerful ability to expose false assumptions and to lead audiences to new thoughts, and profoundly to the truth. We can understand the true (spiritual) side of our nature when abstractions of the truth are presented to us with allegoric examples and stories, for example, Plato's Allegory of the Cave. All of the methods that the ancient Greeks used — inductive and deductive reasoning, logic, allegories, dialectic, unfettered discussion, and stories — are helpful in moving us, God's creatures, back to our spiritual home. Socrates mission was to "sting us out of our forgetfulness", and his playful personality jolted his listeners out of their complacency.

We do not read Plato as we read Holy Writ, however; we peruse his words to obtain pleasure and entertainment and to assist us in honing our clarity of thinking. This life-long quest for an understanding of our human value will lead us to a love of God. We love Plato and his true vision, and Socrates and his virtue, but we do not worship the philosophers; we worship only our Holy God. However, philosophy can sharpen our analytical skills — keep in mind that a logical mind and a spiritual soul are not contradictions; therefore, a brief synopsis of Plato's view of reality will assist us in understanding inductive methodology — a profound tool not only for understanding philosophy but also for the exegesis of the Bible.

In the Allegory of the Cave, Plato imaginatively presents prisoners chained in a cave with their eyes fixed on a wall, where they see only the shadow images of people and things produced from a fire behind them, believing that these semblances are reality.[31] For Plato, the particular shadows that we perceive are copies of reality and through our use of dialectic — will lead the soul back (through clouded senses) to the clarity of vision in the Forms.[32] The universe consists of the world that we experience (empirical), and an immaterial, unperceived one where the objective, transcendent, eternal, intelligible, and archetypal ideals subsist. Ultimate reality depends upon a realm of existing archetypes, all organized beneath the ultimate Form of the Good. When we comprehend this Form through rigorous dialectical thought and discussion, logic, and strict preparation in mathematical studies, the soul will experience excellence, or virtue *(arête)*. Beyond the Forms is the Supreme Soul, who is god, and is the ultimate *arête*.[33] For Plato, god's nature will encompass oneness and goodness, but Plato's disembodied ultimate Form exists without any heart or passions. For Plato, what is good is pleasant and beautiful, pleasing to the eye, and a better proportion of this good thing is intricately patterned — the seeing of which delights. Whatever exists in the world around us was the realization of a Platonic Form. He was a master in the use of symbols and abstract ideas as a place marker or harbinger for the truth, where things remain obscure and abstract to us until we are able to see, read, and understand god's divine alphabet.

Although the Platonic god was not perfect, Plato's concept of a god that is associated with goodness and virtue influenced the ancient Christian converts to look beyond the immediate to the universal. We learn about the perfect, loving, and sacred Christian God who is the source of all goodness and loves us. Plato's god was a disembodied Form that exists without any passions or care for his creation. What is missing in the Platonic god is the profound *agape* love that God has for his creatures. Once we have experienced this energizing and electric force of *agape* love that God has for us, our souls are forever turned toward God's light and love. Plato believed that whatever exists has a proper form, for example, the world around us was the realization of Forms, i.e., the theory of *ontic* logic. Understanding Plato and Socrates' philosophy is crucial to our development as spiritual human beings, but when we learn to exercise our philosophical wings, we want to be trained in the appropriate spiritual territory. For Christians, the world around us is the creation of God; and we participate in this mystery with faith and belief. We see through the glass darkly, but we do understand that we are nourished through the viscosity of the Holiness of our Lord.

We are not setting aside God, but strengthening our resolve to move closer to Him by examining the Platonic Forms or ideals possessed by a group of objects. Each object therefore "copies" or emulates these models for they are eternal and unchanging.

The philosopher is like the prisoner in the cave who is free from his chains and ascends from the cave into the bright sunlight where he realizes that the shadows were not the reality after all. The upward journey of the prisoners from the cave is the journey of the soul from the knowable to the intelligible realm. Socrates tells us, "In the knowable realm, the form of the Good is the last thing to be seen, and it is reached only with difficulty. Once one has seen it, however, one must conclude that it is the cause of all that is correct and beautiful in anything, that it produces both light and its source in the visible realm, and that in the intelligible realm it controls and provides truth and understanding, so that anyone who is to act sensibly in private or public must see it."[34] Socrates taught that education is the turning of one's whole soul toward the brightest thing that he calls the Good. The Socratic philosophy had an energizing force on the minds and lives of those he met, for he was a masterful orator with a powerful spirit and voice. The Hellenistic spirit of seeking out knowledge is with us today as we work toward a better community and nation.

For the ancient Athenians, manly virtue (*arete*) was expected of Athena's male citizens: courage (*andreia*), piety to the gods *(hosiotes)*, temperance in all acts (*sophrosune*), and justice *(dikaiosune)* were the traits exhibited by Athena's men. Like the ancient symbolism of Athena's mascot owl, Socrates' thinking about virtue was more subtle than the popular beliefs. He held that all virtues were in some sense constituted by a certain kind of knowledge: wisdom (*Sophia*). Socrates taught that virtue is knowledge, and any wrongdoing is due to ignorance, and is, therefore, involuntary.[35] Wrongdoing can damage the soul. An ethical failure is the result of a cognitive breakdown, or the result of some false belief about what is good for the person. Both Plato and Aristotle held that there were aspects to virtue that were the result of having one's passions or appetites in the proper order. Socrates also believed that we only desire what is good for us; therefore, his mission was to educate the person about their passions and hungers in order for them to understand, that which is noble.

Humanity's soul (*psyche*) or spirit was developed properly only when each individual kept up a personal quest for knowledge. Individual virtue is what brings us happiness. For Socrates, ignorance is evil, knowledge is good, and an understanding of what is good stimulates a desire for human companionship where we can converse and debate the serious questions of the world with others. Socrates has demonstrated to us that knowledge without virtue is an intellectual aberration, and virtue without knowledge is proof of a moral blindness; therefore, these disjunctions are insufficient for any action toward that which is good. The Platonic City is a morally efficacious society inclusive of knowledge, i.e., for the inhabitants of a good city, virtue is the proper, necessary, and sufficient condition for spiritual growth, health, happiness, beauty, strength and knowledge. Socrates has taught us that our passion for virtue is not to display our goodness to others as a badge of honor, but to act as good people, and to use our rational knowledge for good acts. Socrates states that the soul has a function and if it is to perform its function well, it must possess its own virtue.[36] Socrates teaches us that, "The good person acts well and nobly in what he does, and the one who does well is blessed and happy."[37]

Liberty was not a concept that Socrates taught; however, he taught that individual virtue could bring us complete happiness, and we all search for happiness — in any degree! Socrates' student, Plato, felt that total liberty was not something that we should obtain, and he suggested that those in power used the concept "liberty" to control other people. Plato criticizes the democratic man as one who pursues unfettered freedoms, "And isn't democracies insatiable desire for what it defines as the good also what destroys it?"[38] We march along with Socrates with our passion for virtue — it is a passion for individual freedom (the state of mind where individuals can exercise all of their virtues freely and unencumbered), and philosophy is the handmaiden of freedom (and, freedom is the sister to liberty). As philosophers and citizens of our hypothetical City of the Good, and as discerning human beings we realize that freedom is an axiological idea ready to be shared with the world. This desire for freedom in an open and free society (the Good City) is the appropriate foundation for the activities of free beings, where learning, discussion, debate, an exchange of ideas, unhampered personal and professional growth, can all progress in a positive and enlightened atmosphere. Together, we grow in freedom, where we can clearly see our possibilities for action — without any coercion — our volition to good acts, and can learn more about our individual virtues and reasoning powers. We learn to examine possible activities through the trial of our ideas, and determine if the idea is worthy of an act. We are all representatives of a unique freedom for we have outgrown our adolescent timidity and are now mature in our desire to obtain autonomy.

Through this philosophical pursuit toward real freedom, our accessibility to that which is true will also become more substantial and evident to us as we study and utilize philosophical concepts and precepts. Through knowledge we passionately press away the limitations of our intellect and let our heart and soul discover that which is real, and bypass false notions. The effort of the individual soul, straining toward maturation, gives a history to the person, and through this personal event, the travail in seeing will give birth to what Socrates would call, "the Good". The men and women of the future will each form their own moral consciousness, and will develop a unique intellect and commonality of personhood that knows that individual freedom forms our humanity. As each individual forms a moral foundation as the basis for a genuine freedom, a realization sets in that the world's inhabitants can be blessed to live in freedom. The future of our beautiful earth depends on the awakening consciousness, knowledge, and spiritual growth of each individual, where we can envision and contribute to an earthly paradise.

Socrates is an exceptional spirit whom will assist us on our journey. The philosophical knowledge that he has bequeathed to us has a value far greater than the energy that we will expend learning it. Socrates teaches us to cast a critical eye upon accepted meanings and to question our beliefs as we acquire knowledge, and refine and advance subtle ideas in order to access our unique spiritual dimension. It is our function (as guardians of philosophy) to restore the sensible and rational mode, where ideas are not feared but received in an open-minded spirit and within a progressive public sphere. This philosophical renaissance has a center that takes its paradigm from individual ideas and is metaphysically inseparable from the thematic circuit of ideation. Through the delineation and utilization of axiological ideas, the coarseness of the human nucleus is abolished — and then polished ideational freedom will lead to a physical, material, spiritual and societal freedom. This new birth is initiated by following the Socratic methodological blueprints, which will enable us to be occupied with the mental acquisitions appropriate to the free and inventive development of humankind. These theories are Socratic in that they are the compositional and experimental ideas for the individual, and hence the foundation of society. It is from an acquaintance and relationship with these concepts that the individuals living within a community can develop properly. This Socratic philosophy is not dogmatic but experimental, inquisitive, spiritual, and dialectic.

We will learn more about the historical Socrates and his cognitive theory through the pen of his most famous pupil, Plato, when we turn next to the pages of the *Republic*. In the *Republic*, Plato develops his own tripartite theory of the soul, but we still — clearly and distinctly — hear the voice of his master, Socrates!

CHAPTER SIX

The Republic: The Good City

Through the pen and pages of Plato, we read Socrates' philosophy, and emulate his life and actions as our philosophical model. Announced by the Archangel Gabriel, the Holy Nazarene taught us the truth of God's Divine Word, and we learn that even the wisest of us are novices in the Kingdom of God. Both men were teachers of virtue and both men worked tirelessly to promote virtue in others. Socrates taught using dialectic, i.e., question and answer, and Jesus taught in a didactic and authoritative manner using parables and prophecy to reveal His divine mission. Our human rights are bestowed upon us by our Holy God, as the inspiration for our republican form of government, whereby, we, as citizens, take it upon ourselves to act responsibly in our mission to safeguard our freedoms. Our justice, liberty, equality and freedom are the rational outcome of our laws (based upon the common history, heritage, and development of British common law), and are always in harmony with God's commandments for us. Our mistakes, and disharmony within God's Providence for us, will be corrected by our increased wisdom and knowledge of our comings and goings (and hope) for placement within our Father's House.

Ancient Greek philosophy taught the logos of the gods; the Hebrew Scriptures taught the Logos of God. "And the Word became flesh, and dwelt among us, and we saw His glory as of the only begotten from the Father, full of grace and truth" (1 John 1:14). The ancient philosophers were instructed by wisdom, reason, lessons from a pantheon of gods, and *logos* (which was the written word for the ancient Greeks); and Socrates had his *daimonen,* which has often been characterized as his inner voice or spiritual *logos*. There is an intellectual journey over the span of time between Socrates' teaching the truth of the immortality of the soul, virtue and justice, Plato's teaching the eternity of "Ideas", and the "Forms", to Jesus' divine teaching, and the current impartation of the Holy Word. However, all of this knowledge and wisdom, and our sojourn on this earth, lead us on the path to the ineffable God. For spiritual natures — improved over the celestial epoch — we are active within our sphere for the good of the Sacred Kingdom.

For the ancient Athenians, politics and religion were inextricable practices within a polis of active citizens who formed the first democracy. The ancient Athenian culture worshiped the extraordinary man epitomized by a pantheon of gods, for example, Zeus, Jupiter, and Juno. The ancient Greeks relied on the common cultural heritage of Homer's *Iliad* and *The Odyssey* written by

Homer, (approximately late eighth or early seventh century B.C.), where the adventures of the extraordinary man are told in colorful, imaginative, and beautiful poetry. *The Illiad* is an epic poem about Ilium (Troy) that recounts the Achaean attack on Troy, and the rage of Achilles, and the consequences of his rage. Achilles (described as very quick and strong with a prowess in war and possessing a godlike beauty), was the son of a mortal father and an immortal mother. He was portrayed as a larger than life person who wrestled with the decision to either lay siege to Troy and insure his glory (*kleos*) as a conquering hero, or sail home where his glory and pride will die. In *The Odyssey,* the hero Odysseus makes his ten-year journey home after the military campaign in which the Greeks destroy the non-Greek city of Troy. The Olympian gods were a quarrelsome lot who lacked morality, compassion, or predictability, and did not exhibit the Socratic virtues. The Homeric gods, for example, are intrusive, disruptive, jealous, angry, competitive, and passionate personages and the ancient Athenians occupied a lot of their time worshipping these entities for appeasement in order to live a blessed life. The goddess Athena appears in Greek mythology as the patron of many heroes, including Odysseus and Heracles. In *The Odyssey*, Odysseus' shrewdness won Athena's favor as she guided him on his long journey home to win back his kingdom.

Athena, or Pallas Athena, was the patron goddess of human ingenuity and resourcefulness in handicrafts and skill in human relationships. Athena was one of the most powerful goddesses of ancient Greece — who bequeathed the olive tree to Athens — was always successful in her battles, and was the goddess of wisdom, and learning. As a patron of Athens, Athena fought in the Trojan War on the side of the Achaeans, Athena only fought for a reasonable cause and much preferred to use intuitive wisdom (or cunning intelligence) rather than force or violence. Alongside the image of Athena in Plato's dialogue the *Timaeus*, Plato envisioned the Supreme Soul and a hierarchy of emanations from the supreme reality of the divine. Although the Platonic Dialogues are filled with images of the pantheon of Greek gods, Plato conceived God's nature as oneness, goodness, and transcendence. The intelligible forms cannot be reduced to the things in the spatio-temporal world, but these abstractions do not exist in isolation from the things on Earth. Mathematical abstractions are the permanent entities within the flux — mathematical forms make nature intelligible to us, as they are immanent in nature.

In the *Republic*, Book VII, Socrates teaches Glaucon the importance of geometry in war where the strategy of "setting up camp, occupying a region, concentrating troops, deploying them, or with regard to any of the other formations an army adopts in battle or on the march, it makes all the difference whether someone is a geometer or not." Socrates speculates whether or not advanced geometry will "make it easier to see the form of the good." He searched for mathematical proportions in nature, geometry, astronomy, harmonics, medical theories, and optics. Plato and his students sought the mathematical beauty of truth and to enter his Academy, an advanced facility with mathematics was required.[39]

Classical Athenians were active citizens, and the citizen body made up the polis, where the ancient Greeks were constructing a government of justice based upon the laws of Solon instead of the involvement of the pantheon of gods. The Homeric values of individual renown *(kleos)* (and extraordinary feats performed by men who were assisted by the gods and goddesses) evolved to a higher moral measure with Socratic values. Socrates' mission was to teach his fellow Athenians to care for their souls, so his mission is very relevant to our modern goal of individual self-improvement. Jesus' Holy Mission on earth centered on the Kingdom of God, and opened the hearts of believers. Jesus taught us to behave as if the Kingdom of God had arrived, and God's Kingdom is a City of justice and equity, so for believers politics and religion are inextricable. We place full confidence in God's Word and worship His Holiness, and are thankful for His love, grace and the gift of salvation. Unlike Socrates' wisdom (which we can study and debate), we cannot fully understand God's wisdom, but we do know that his supernatural peace encompasses justice and equity. Therefore, our study of Plato's *Republic* (which defines justice) will advance our understanding of this concept and through this exegesis, we will then begin to understand divine justice. As we study Plato's *Republic*, we remember, "the peace of God, which surpasses all comprehension, will guard your hearts and your minds in Christ Jesus" (Phil 4:7).

The *Republic* is the most well-known of the Platonic books, and the *Republic* is a city that Plato creates, but does not actually exist. Plato wrote the *Republic* approximately 380 B.C., where he represents an authoritarian society ruled by a "philosopher-king", and dominated by an elite class of "guardians". Keep in mind that Plato wrote the *Republic* after the execution of Socrates, so the tragic loss of his teacher must have influenced Plato's criticism of democracy as a form of government. In the *Republic,* the main narrator, Socrates, asks the question, what is justice? Socrates defines justice, the character of a just city-state, and the just man. Socrates examines this question within the context of the political communities, and in terms of the individual person or soul. Plato constructs a city in order to examine this virtue, and then (through Socrates' personae) he illustrates it by the analogy of justice in the human soul. One of the driving questions of the dialogue: is the just person happier than the unjust person? We read the *Republic,* and learn that Socrates taught that virtue promotes happiness, and knowledge is necessary for virtue. In the *Republic,* Socrates considers a range of subjects to defend the just life: rival theories of justice, competing views of human happiness, education, philosophy, the role of philosophers, virtues and vices, the good and bad souls, political regimes, the structure of reality, the Forms, and the role of women and of art in society.

Although we do not live in a utopia like Plato's *Republic*, there are many things that we can learn from the philosophy contained within this Book because it is a utopia based upon the development of the individual soul. Socrates taught us to understand and develop our own soul and spiritual identity, (although 'spiritual identity' are not words that Socrates would use, the concept of the development of the soul remains the same for him as it is for us today), and in doing so we will then nurture and facilitate the society that we live in. The complexity of the individual human lends itself to an enlightened understanding of the soul, and spiritual individuals respect others, exhibit a high degree of love for family members, are independent, serve community and faith, set goals of achievement, recognize and practice equality, are peace-makers, seek happiness and fulfillment, and understand the value of freedom.

In America, for example, our constitutional republic was designed to give maximum freedom to the citizens in all areas of their individual private and public lives, and their social, religious, and political endeavors. Our nation's Founders believed in God's Holy guidance in the creation of our Republic, and the fervent prayer of modern Christians is that God continues to bless our nation with His Holy protection. Although our Constitution provides for the separation of Church and State, individual citizens are entitled to their own beliefs, and for many, politics and religion are inextricable. We reflect upon Jesus' mission, where politics and religion were united, for example, when Jesus overturned the moneychangers' tables and said to them, "It is written, 'My house shall be called a house of prayer'; but you are making it a robbers' den" (Mat 21:13). Jesus taught us that our community is based upon Christian faith when He revealed to us the Holiness of the Kingdom of God. In the world of Socrates, the city was part of a religious community in a way that is not recognized in our secular society, but for modern believers, we behave as if the

Kingdom of God were at hand, and the privilege of being a citizen in a democracy is reflected in our worship of the Lord.

The ancient Athenian civic life was intertwined with their personal devotion to the gods. The events in Book I take place on the festival day of the goddess Bendis (Artemis) at the Pireaus (where nonresident aliens live), and in the house of Cephalus. We get an idea of Socrates' charm and intellectual gifts when Polemarchus and the other men ask Socrates to accompany them for the pleasure of his company. The main characters are Socrates, Cephalus, Polemarchus, and Thrasymachus. Cephalus (Polymarchus' father) welcomes Socrates and says, "Socrates you don't come down to the Piraeus to see us as often as you should..., you ought to come here more often, for you should know that as the physical pleasures wither away, my desire for conversation and its pleasures grow."[40] Socrates engages Cephalus (who was a wealthy merchant and businessman) with a dialogue on the subject of aging. Cephalus tells Socrates that the loss of youthful vigor is pleasantly liberating. Socrates suggests that Cephalus' attitude may be because of his personal wealth and the comfort that wealth brings. Cephalus does not believe that justice is necessary for happiness, but tells Socrates that wealth does give you peace of mind in facing the afterlife. "When someone thinks that the end is near," says Cephalus, "he becomes frightened and concerned about things he didn't fear before. It's then that the stories we're told about Hades, about how people who've been unjust here must pay the penalty there..."[41] From the merits of old age and the material comforts that wealth can bring, Cephalus tells Socrates that justice is living up to your legal obligations and being honest. Socrates refutes Cephalus' definition of justice (*dikaiosyne*), i.e., speaking the truth and paying back debts. The Greek term *dikaiosyne* is translated as justice or right, and it means "right behavior" and, for Plato, justice is a matter of taking care of one's own — or minding one's own — business, whatever it may be.

After Cephalus and Socrates agree that truth-telling and paying back debts is not a definition of justice, Cephalus (who earlier professed a love of conversation) leaves the discussion, and Polemarchus takes up the task, defining justice as giving a man what he deserves. Polemarchus says that if we are to believe the poet Simonides (who was considered to be wise and god-like), then it is just to give to each what is due to him. Socrates further questions Polemarchus who clarifies his position by adding that while it is just to do good to friends; however, you owe your enemies harm, but must never cause injury to your allies. Socrates counters stating that people often make mistakes, thinking an enemy a friend and vice versa, thus the just man could unintentionally help enemies and harm his friends. At this point, Socrates, as he often did, appeals to the notion of a craft (*techne*), which covers any skill or activity requiring specialized knowledge, making references to farmers, physicians, a ship's pilot, etc. who are all capable of benefiting their friends and yet harming their adversaries. A skilled doctor is very good at healing people, and keeping them alive, however, he could also be proficient at killing them (if so inclined), so is he just? Polemarchus responds that a just man is most capable of benefiting friends and harming enemies in waging war and alliances. Socrates then questions, how are those not at war to be helped by the just person, and Polemarchus replies that justice helps one use or acquire contracts. Socrates then asks Polemarchus if what he means by contracts is partnerships, and Polemarchus responds yes. Socrates follows by inquiring, what special areas of expertise ethical persons have to make them helpful in contracts and Polemarchus states that they are accommodating with money matters, and are best at keeping money and other items safe by guarding them. Socrates replies, "If a just person is clever at guarding money, therefore, he must also be clever at stealing it".[42] Polemarchus — in the clutches of Socrates examination — admits, "I don't know any more what I did mean, but I still believe that to benefit one's friends and harm one's enemies is justice".[43] Socrates returns that we could be mistaken about who is good and useful, and the same could hold true for our enemies. Polemarchus then offers, clarifying his position, "Someone who is both believed to be useful and is useful is a friend; someone who is believed to be useful but isn't, is believed to be a friend but isn't. And the same for the enemy."[44] Socrates asks Polemarchus, "When someone is harmed do they become worse in human virtue *(arête)?*" Socrates defines justice as human virtue; therefore, he concludes that, "people who are harmed must become more unjust". Socrates concludes that, "it isn't the function of a just person to harm a friend or anyone else; rather it is the function of his opposite, an unjust person".[45]

Polemarchus still contends that justice is to benefit one's friends and harm one's enemies, yet Socrates argues that we could misidentify our friends and enemies, and due to this error in judgement, end up injuring comrades and aiding our foes.[46] Socrates asks, "Is it, then, the role of a just man to harm anyone?"[47]

Thrasymachus, agitated by the discussion, "coiled himself up like a wild beast about to spring, and he hurled himself at us as if to tear us to pieces."[48] Thrasymachus yelled at Socrates, "Give an answer yourself, and tell us what you say the just is,...tell me clearly and exactly what you mean; for I won't accept such nonsense from you."[49] Socrates responded that he never claimed to have the answer, and when an eminent man like Thrasymachus forbids him to express his opinion, it is better if Thrasymachus gives his own thoughts on the topic. Thrasymachus defines justice as the interest of the stronger, that we can understand as "might makes right." Socrates points out that the stronger may not always know his own interest. Socrates states that a ruler acts in the best interest of his subjects, and a physician acts in the best interest of his patients, as well as a captain for his crew. Then the debate contrasts tyranny or perfect injustice, with the benevolent rule or perfect justice. The unjust man has pride and ambition, which can be weaknesses, whereas, the just man has humility, wisdom and strength.

Socrates argues in favor of the just life over the unjust by claiming that a just person is good and clever, and an unjust one is ignorant and bad.⁵⁰ Socrates further argues for the just life by stating that injustice produces internal disharmony, which will prevent effective actions. Justice is a soul's virtue when it performs its function well, and a person performing the various functions of the soul well is a happier person.⁵¹

As the discussion comes to an end in Book I, Socrates points out that Simonides did not hold the view that justice is helping friends and harming enemies, (more likely that is the view of wealthy tyrants who believe that might will make right). Socrates points out that the aim of a man's life should be justice not injustice, and he uses the analogy of the soul and its proper functions to prove his argument. If the soul's end is life, and the execution of that end is fulfillment of life, then justice is the excellence of the soul, and therefore, the just man enjoys a better quality of life. The main conclusion is that justice is the excellence of the soul, yet Socrates concludes that he still knows nothing about the nature of justice. He states that an adequate account of justice is necessary before they can decide whether the just life is better than the unjust one.⁵²

Thrasymachus, Polymarchus, and the others leave to enjoy the festival, and Socrates continues the discussion on justice with Glaucon and Adeimantus in Book II. Glaucon distinguishes between things that are good in themselves and things that are good for their consequences.⁵³ Glaucon says to Socrates, "I think that Thrasymachus gave up before he had to, charmed by you as if he were a snake. But I'm not yet satisfied by the argument on either side. I want to know what justice and injustice are and what power each itself has when it's by itself in the soul."[54] Glaucon plays devil's advocate in order to resolve the debate and states that justice is a legally enforced compromise between doing injustice to others or having injustice done to oneself. He shares an allegory where a shepherd puts on an invisible ring, and when he recognized its power he seduced the queen of the kingdom, killed the king (with the help of the queen), and took over the kingdom.[55] Glaucon's analogy suggests that if we were free from all legal and social responsibility, then any man would seek his own power and act unjustly. Glaucon's brother, Adeimantus, recites poetry from Aeschylus, Hesiod, and Homer that endorse the rewards of injustice, and the ease of vice, over justice. Adeimantus argues that the unjust person with the appearance or reputation of being just will be happier than the just person.[56]

Socrates is asked to defend this concept for itself and not for the reputation, it allows for.[57] He begins the discussion with the origins of political life, and a city that satisfies the basic human necessities. Socrates proposes to "watch a city coming to be in theory, wouldn't we also see its justice coming to be, and its injustice as well?"[58] Therefore, Socrates and his companions create a city, the *Republic*, in theory from its beginnings, with the needs of humankind — food, shelter, and clothes — taken into consideration. Each man in the city would be assigned a single occupation that suits his natural talents and inclinations. Plato is interested in the ideal State, that is, what a state ought to be if it is to conform to the pattern of the Forms. The State must contain justice, along with wisdom, courage, and temperance, which will be found in the three classes in this perfect city: guardians, soldiers, and producers. The predominant elements found in these three classes are the thinking element (wisdom) in the guardians, courage in the soldiers, and temperance is found in all three classes. The principles of justice are the virtues found in the individual soul, as well as the virtues found in classes within the State. Justice is the virtue that enables all of these qualities to thrive, where each class can accomplish the task for which it is best suited. The care of the soul is the primary goal for living well, and as all three classes strive for this, there is a harmony within the whole State.

In Book III, Socrates teaches that the individual who has the most developed reason and wisdom should be the ruler. This philosopher-king should act as sovereign for they not only have experience, education, and superior judgement; they hold true knowledge of the Forms, including the Form of the Good, which contains justice.[59] Plato writes that these traits found in one person is unlikely (although not impossible), therefore, he proposes a method of rule by a group that he calls the guardians, who would have harmonious arrangements with the reasoning parts of their soul. Plato's myth of metals is proposed in order to convince everyone to accept his or her position in the city: the rulers have gold, the guardians have silver, and the producers will have bronze.[60]

In Book IV, Socrates states that the city is completely good and virtuous, and therefore it is wise, courageous, moderate, and just.[61] The reasoning, spirited, and desiring (appetitive part) elements found within the soul of the individual correspond to the virtues found within the three classes in the city.[62] These three aspects of the soul correspond to the three classes within the state: reason corresponds to the rulers, emotions, or spirited things to the auxiliaries, and desire or passions correspond to the craftsmen.[63] The Four Cardinal Virtues within the individual are wisdom, courage, temperance, and justice. When man is exercising his reason, he can achieve wisdom; when he displays his emotions or spirit, he has courage; when reason rules over his emotions and desires, a man will display his temperance; and when reason rules over the emotions and spirited elements and rules over the desires and passions, justice will be secured.

Plato interrupts the Socratic argument about justice to defend some of the features of the ideal city. Book V shows that knowledge requires an understanding of the Forms. The philosophers are lovers of the truth and are able to see the beautiful itself "in its own right" (*kath'hauto*).[64] Those of us who rely solely on our sight of sensible things will accept beautiful things, shapes, colors, objects, but we are never able to see the beautiful itself. In Book VI, Socrates teaches his epistemology with an analogy of the divided line. True knowledge begins with reasoning from premise and hypothesis involving mathematical entities, and culminates in pure thought or dialectic. The Platonic epistemology (the study of the nature and validity of knowledge) and ontology (the study of existence and the methods of discovering those truths) are bound together. Therefore, true knowledge of changing sensible objects is impossible, for each person experiences their own reality and develops their own theories of their world. If an individual utilizes the mind, an individual will have intellectual knowledge regarding the world of Forms, as perceived through a dialectical process of reasoning. Our soul is affected by a clarity and truth through the partaking of the Platonic Forms without the utilization of the senses, for they (mathematical, ethical, and physical ideals) subsist in a metaphysical realm and are eternal, uncreated, and immutable.

In Book VI, Plato writes that philosophers should rule the city because they are better able to know the truth and they have the relevant practical knowledge needed to reign. As patterns for the individuals in the sensible world, the Forms are the absolute standards of judgment. The philosopher loves what *is* (the Forms), not what is becoming (the world of senses). For example, if one is asked to indicate justice, and replies that justice is a certain set of laws, being unaware of the Form of justice, then this individual is in a state of opinion regarding it. However, after education, training, and the utilization of the dialectical process of reasoning, this individual can apprehend justice in itself. Socrates teaches that both men and women are both naturally suited to the task of guardians.[65]

Justice itself subsists within the Form of the Good, and when one learns this, and then he/she is in a state of true knowledge. Plato assumes that the Forms, that is, the true being or essence of things: justice, beauty, and goodness are unchanging, indestructible, and incorruptible. The Platonic conception of sensible things as copies of the unchanging Forms entails that any change will tend toward corruption in proportion to the movement that leads away from the participation in the Forms. Knowledge is of a stable object, and opinion is of objects or things that are becoming and changing appearances. A philosopher has knowledge of the single Forms, they love and pursue wisdom, and they love the sight of truth.[66]

Socrates was a powerful spirit with a masterful voice and a message for freedom of speech (*parrhesia*). He had an energizing effect on the lives of those he met, and even today, he energizes us with ideas of liberty *(eleutheria)*, and people-power *(demos-kratia)*. The Hellenistic spirit of seeking out knowledge is with us today as we work toward improving our souls. Ancient Athenian democracy changed in character after the humiliating defeat by the Spartans and large loss of lives in the Peloponnesian War. Athens entered into a period of uncertainty about its identity; a period of instability where plebiscitarian excesses could lead to the execution of Socrates, their greatest defender of the rule of law against emotionalism. In the same way that our western democracy is evolving from the emotionalism of the past to a moral reliance on the rule of law and the vision of individualism that activates our representative government. Socrates' concern was always for the rule of law in Athens, and the development of the soul of its citizens.

In Book VII, Socrates teaches his students the Allegory of the Cave (discussed on pages 98-101), which represents the philosopher's education and ascent from ignorance to knowledge of the Forms. The chained prisoners do not know that they are confined in a cave, and that they can be free to understand things in the intelligible realm. Education directs the rational faculties (the "divine attributes" 518d-519a), and with the proper training we can perceive the Form of the Good. The upward journey of the prisoners from the cave is the journey of the soul from the knowable to the intelligible realm. Socrates teaches Glaucon that the Form of the Good "is the cause of all that is correct and beautiful in anything, that it produces both light and its source in the visible realm, and that in the intelligible realm it controls and provides truth and understanding."[67] Once the philosopher views the Forms, he/she must descend back into the darkness of the cave in order to teach others (521c-d) to find "the being itself of each thing" (532a).

Underlying Socrates' moral examination was his religious commitment — he believed that an intelligent being was behind the construction of the universe. He taught that the gods were superior to us in power and wisdom. The majority of the ancient Greeks, however, imposed limitations on divine power. Socrates, however, did not believe that the gods were limited (or that they had the faults that were portrayed in the ancient myths). He taught that the material body was greedy for pleasure and the satisfaction of material things. The immortal soul was the moral aspect of the person, and could be trained to recognize and understand virtue, thus, applying this knowledge to daily living. Knowledge, virtue, and wisdom are related, and Socrates examined these areas in others, using the art of question and answer. Centuries later, Jesus used this same method to stimulate His listeners to think and search within their own souls for the truth. We will examine the similarities between the dialectical style of Christ and Socrates. Through Socratic philosophy, we will deepen our spiritual understanding.

Socrates was born during an era of polytheism and superstition, but he taught that virtues could assist us in becoming better human beings. For example, Plato states that there is only one thing that makes an object beautiful, namely, its association with absolute Beauty.[68] These Forms or ideals (including Beauty) are eternal and unchanging with everything whether empirical or theoretical, dependent upon their existence. Many problems with modern thinkers stem from the fact that they identify with numerous particulars, but not with universal concepts, like these Platonic archetypes.

For Socrates, the proper education and training is to turn the rational part of the soul toward what it needs to see, so the soul will then pursue the right ends.[69] Socrates taught that education is the turning of one's whole soul toward the brightest thing that he calls the Good. The released prisoner from the cave, who has looked upon and contemplated the true light of the sun, must return to the cave for the duty of ruling the other prisoners. The enlightened one has new eyes ill fitted for cave life, and will be mocked by the other captives. The guardians must give up the beauty of the light in order to rule for the common good, for they have spent fifty years in preparation for this honor, and Socrates feels that they will gladly make the sacrifice for their fellow citizens. The guardians, and those who will eventually become philosopher-kings, will be educated in poetry, music, and physical education.[70] Then there is further education in mathematics that includes arithmetic and numbers,[71] plane geometry,[72] and solid geometry:[73] following mathematics is a study of astronomy,[74] and harmonics.[75] Then the philosophers will study dialectic that, "gently pulls the eye of the soul out and leads it upwards"[76] to understand the Forms and the highest Form of the Good. Socrates taught that there was a higher vision of reality than the one that we immediately know and experience. The philosopher (who has had the vision of the Form of the Good) will understand the harmony of all parts of the universe, and, therefore, understand virtue, which is the harmony of the human soul with the universe of Ideas and the knowledge of one's true self. This virtue will ensure order, harmony, and intelligence, and stimulate a pattern to a soul, which has its being within a world that is in flux. Socrates believed that the soul could be stimulated to awaken consciousness and develop moral character. For Socrates, the ascending vision of that which is Good is to be strived for above all else.

Socrates taught that the principles of justice are fundamental for the maintenance of the state. The ontology is a world of Forms, and that which is real being as opposed to our physical world of becoming. Knowledge of the Form of the Good is the highest truth, which contains the essence of justice. For the classes within the state, justice is defined as the harmonious inter-relationship of three classes, i.e., guardians, soldiers, and producers. On the individual level, justice is defined as the harmonious correlation of the three elements in the soul, i.e., reasoning, spirited, and desiring elements. It is interesting that the larger — the just city — will not differ from the smaller, the just man. The likeness between the city and the man is that virtue called justice.

In Book VIII, Socrates analyzes the forms of corrupt government, with the goal of looking at the individuals who live in these governments in order to find the just man. The four principle forms of defective government are timocracy, oligarchy, democracy, and tyranny. The aristocracy (the Republic) will degenerate into a timocracy if there is an error in population control. The just individual degenerates into the timocratic person when the spirited part of the soul overpowers rationality and then an ambitious, combative nature will arise. The timocracy is based on honor and not justice, and the ruler ingratiates himself to those who flatter him. When wealth becomes the standard, an oligarchy will develop. The oligarchic individual has a desiring part of the soul that takes over the reasoning and spirited part, and the outcome is an unbenevolent, pleasure-loving man. The democratic state arises when appetites instead of reason or honor sway the ruler. The democratic man casts off all restraints, liberates all the unnecessary desires, and becomes a spendthrift. Democracy is a poor political system because the state would be in the hands of people who do not have the knowledge or skills to rule. Socrates questioned the soundness of Athens democracy, and maintained that it was not the buildings or the warships that make this form of government great, but the soul of the democrat that gives it distinction.

Socrates talks about the tyrant in depth in Book IX. A tyranny arises when democracy has unlimited freedom and no morals. The tyrant begins by promising to release people from debt, but by the end of the tyrants' reign, he has taxed the people into poverty and slavery. The tyrant has ungovernable appetites, and because the despot is a strong man who is a slave to fear, he feels threatened by assassination and betrayal. Socrates again asks the question whether the unjust man who is perceived as just in the public is better or worse than the just man who is perceived as unjust. Socrates concludes that whether or not the ideal state becomes a reality, the philosopher must live as if it were real inside him.

In the final book of the Republic, Book X, Socrates assesses the poetic arts, and leaves those out of the ideal state unless they portray nobility and right behavior. The poet is an imitator who knows nothing about what a thing is in itself, and therefore has no knowledge of the truth. This is a harsh criticism by our philosopher, as we know that the creative arts stimulate our lives and give quality to our perceptions in their "imitation" or portrayal of the truth. Socrates tells the Myth of Er to illustrate reward and punishment of souls in the afterlife.[77] Er is a brave soldier who dies in battle, but comes back to life to tell the story of his adventure after his soul has left his body. Each departed soul is allowed to pick the sort of life that he will lead and some choose wisely while others do not. After choosing their new lives, they drink from the River of Forgetfulness so that they will not come back and tell what they have seen and heard. True recompense arises when the just man reaps the rewards of leading a moral life, and is welcomed by the gods in the afterlife. He is blessed with immortality for his soul, as he is born once more into another existence. Socrates states, "...that the soul is immortal and able to endure every evil and every good, and we'll always hold to the upward path, practicing justice with reason in every way".[78]

Plato argues that justice alone does not secure happiness, however, the just person can expect to achieve bliss now and in the afterlife, once justice secures the external goods through society or the favor of the gods, therefore, justice contributes to contentment. Socrates taught that we should always side with justice and never do injustice (*adikein*) to anyone. When the Thirty Tyrants ordered Socrates to arrest Leon of Salamis, Socrates refused and calmly went home because he knew that Leon was innocent.[79] We admire the integrity of Socrates who was committed to the quality of our understanding of what to care about and to just action. Socrates lived and died by his beliefs — at the age of seventy, he was charged with impiety (for offending the Olympian gods — Apollo and Zeus). After a lifelong pursuit of philosophizing and piously following Apollo (through his oracle at Delphi), he faced representatives of the democratic people of Athens to defend himself against charges of corrupting the young. "Very well then, men of Athens, I must surely defend myself and attempt to uproot from your minds in so short a time the slander that has resided there so long."[80] Plato writes, "The jury now gave its verdict of guilty, and Meletus asks for the penalty of death".[81] Socrates tells the gentlemen of the jury, "keep this one truth in mind, that a good man cannot be harmed either in life or in death,..."[82]

Despite the philosophical stain on the Athenians for putting Socrates to death, they had a personal relationship with their new democracy that can be considered to exist on a deeper level than we do today; they believed that the gods sanctioned their government. Each citizen participated when his *deme* lot was chosen, and vigorously debated the ideas that created the free city of Athens. There was no separation between the secular and the sacred; religion was vital to the polis and the rituals to please the gods in word and deed were part of the social fabric of the Athenian state. The belief in a pantheon of gods evolved to the belief in One Supreme God with the birth and teaching of Jesus Christ and the spread of Christianity. Although we no longer believe in a pantheon of gods, we can benefit from wisdom's life giving force of spirit. This author is not suggesting that we abandon our separation of church and state, however, citizens with a heightened sense of the spirituality of their souls can only benefit the whole community. Further, we can certainly make use of the Athenian notion of *parrhesia* (the freedom of citizens to openly express their personal views in the public square), for an enlightened democracy will advocate for its citizens to engage in a free exchange of ideas. Granted, we do not live in Socrates' ideal city, but we can listen to what Socrates instructed us to do, and that is to care for our souls and to live a good life. Socrates urged us to imagine this city as if it were real inside of us! We can live our lives as if we are living in a good city, and a good nation; and, if we find one good soul, then there will be two and then three, and then many, many more that will band together with the common Socratic goal: to care for one's soul. We can live as if the human race of philosophers will take one long stride across our city, and with acute measurement calibrate what is needed to bring together individuals with virtuous souls who can live in fellowship with reason and just laws.

Therefore, we can live as if all the decadence will remain outside the walls of the Socratic polis. Our spiritual hunger is satisfied within the new city where a hierarchy of gifts and giftedness of soul will be accomplished by each member of the community. A transfiguration from active human being to activity of the spirit on the highest level can therefore take place by each member of this city by virtue of whom they are. Our aspirations are to separate ourselves away from evil and anchor ourselves in the good. Our current love for materialism has divided our minds and hearts, and this division is repaired through the Socratic healing of the soul. Our self-determination in spirit is the balm for curing this disease of materialism, and we make a personal affirmation of the holiness of our existence. Socrates has guided us on our journey, and has provided us with a map of where we may now travel for our own self-determination and spiritual growth.

Socrates teaches the hierarchy of the immortal soul over the body in the *Republic, Phaedo, Craytlus,* and the *Laws.* In the *Craytlus,* Socrates teaches his friend Hermogenes, "Thus some people say that the body *(soma)* is the tomb *(sema)* of the soul, on the grounds that it is entombed in its present life, while others say that it is correctly called 'a sign' *(sema)* because the soul signifies whatever it wants to signify by means of the body. I think it is most likely the followers of Orpheus who gave the body its name, with the idea that the soul is being punished for something and that the body is an enclosure or prison in which the soul is securely kept *(sozetai)*—as the name *'soma' itself* suggests—until the penalty is paid; for, on this view, not even a single letter of the word need to be changed."[83] During Socrates lifetime, the art of etymology was often practiced and, of course, Socrates was an acute analyzer of names. Socrates held (unlike his contemporaries) that the nature of reality was not in a state of flux, and to learn the truth about names meant that you had to grasp the permanent unchanging nature of things as they are in the Platonic Forms.

The Platonic theory of the immortality of the soul was necessary for divine justice, where the good souls met their reward and the evil ones could expect punishment after life. The profound idea that individuals had an eternal soul and a divine spirit beyond the material body was a concept that influenced the development of early Christian thinking about the after-life. Early Jewish discussion about God was primarily concerned with the immediate life — what happens to God's people on the earth. The Platonic ideology in the form of Neo-Platonism bridged the conceptual enlightenment from the pagan culture to the Hebrew-Christian cultures. The

Apostle Paul preached that the buried body of Jesus was transformed by the Pneuma of God (*soma pneumatikon*), and the disciples witnessed the transformed body of Christ. For the early Christians, the apotheosis of Jesus' soul to the divine realm would be understood by early Christians who had an understanding of an immortal soul, but the resurrection of Jesus' body was more difficult to grasp, but came to be understood through faith, witness, God's Holy Word, and the Holy Spirit. The Divine Justice of the Holy Lord will transform our bodies and our earth. Paul taught the believers at Thessalonia, "For after all it is only just for God to repay with affliction those who afflict you, and to give relief to you who are afflicted and to us as well when the Lord Jesus will be revealed from heaven with His mighty angels in flaming fire, dealing out retribution to those who do not know God and to those who do not obey the gospel of our Lord Jesus. These will pay the penalty of eternal destruction, away from the presence of the Lord and from the glory of His power, when He comes to be glorified in His saints on that day and to be marveled at among all who have believed — for our testimony to you was believed" (2 Thess 1:6-10). Our vigils burn bright as our prayers are answered for the return of the Holy Lord and the Divine Justice that will transform our earthly bodies, and our earth for the return of God's golden age.

We learn from the *Republic* that Socrates had the notion of the justice of the soul and the city, i.e., the rational control over the spirited versus the appetites of the soul. A harmonious city (as well as an individual behaving in harmony with a good soul) is where the citizens are performing their designated functions. The soul, upon its death, would descend into Hades where it was judged and reborn to another human cycle of reincarnation, where ideally it could ascend to a higher realm free from the imperfections of the physical world. For Christians, the essential self will be resurrected with a new immortal body that frees it from the Greek Hadean state of death. Paul taught the ancient Greeks in the cosmopolitan city of Corinth, "Now I say this, brethren, that flesh and blood cannot inherit the kingdom of God; nor does the perishable inherit the imperishable" (1 Cor 15:50).

Socratic wisdom has lovingly brought us to the justice of God where our victory awaits us. He taught justice (*dikaiosune*), and justice is one of the main themes of God's Holy Word. Socrates' ideal city was harmonious when all of the soul-functions of the inhabitants were performing according to their design, and (similarly) the Christian City is harmonious when our souls are functioning according to God's design for us. Justice is a relationship between the individual and God, and then reflected in the community. God's Agape Love and Holiness fulfill our spiritual growth through God's covenant with His children as the promise of the New Jerusalem unfolds where we will live nourished. "For a child will be born to us, a son will be given to us; And the government will rest on His shoulders; And His name will be called Wonderful Counselor, Mighty God, Eternal Father, Prince of Peace. There will be no end to the increase of His government or of peace, On the throne of David and over his kingdom, To establish it and to uphold it with justice and righteousness From then on and forevermore. The zeal of the Lord of hosts will accomplish this" (Isa 9:6-7). As workers toward this goal of God's City, we are stirred to action by our zeal for the job at hand. Our labor is to construct a city whose function is that which is good. The task will be accomplished by our reason, faith, and action. When you reach a certain level of abstract reasoning a rational faith fits in when we begin to think about those areas where we do not have any physical access. Our goal is spiritual growth, and our current workshop is the material world where hierarchies of gifted individuals are actively seeking out that which is good.

Through the study of philosophy, we learn that the soul is nourished through the understanding of that which is holy. There is some measure of mundane divinity in Plato, and certainly Socrates, and we are attracted to their spiritually radiant mental light where we discover the illumination of the truth. However, the wisdom of philosophy is not the wisdom of God, "but when we speak God's wisdom in a mystery, the hidden wisdom which God predestined before the ages to our glory; the wisdom which none of the rulers of this age has understood; for if they had understood it they would not have crucified the Lord of glory" (1 Cor 2:7-8). Our spiritual selves are hidden under the protective cloak of God's mystery (and trembling under His glory): the lambs must not go unfed!

God's Spirit upon our hearts seals our inheritance as children of Christ, and our realization of our birthright as children of God unfolds to us in stages. Just as Socrates taught us that we come to a knowledge of ourselves through the utilization of our soul functions, we remember that God has anointed us to be a portion of the Christ-family. Our soul (which this author calls our holy quiddity) is a unique and intensive configuration that is a specific composition of each unique individual. The integrity of this composition is a pre-established and holy impregnation, for the purpose of a human and spiritual Christ-like attainment. Human nature exhibits itself as being holy in the specific Christ-like acts, the performance of which will give the individual certainty that the mystery of God is performed through our humble acts of attainment. We function as both reasoning and spiritual beings of God, unique as to its actuation in union of His Holiness. What is even more real than the notion of humanity is the idea of a holy humanity being born again to populate His Sacred City. Our souls are not tattered, but wrapped as golden sheaths around our loving hearts that belong only to the Lord.

CHAPTER SEVEN

The Spirit of Freedom is Upon the Earth

A covenant of hope and desire will bind the material world to the spiritual for an embodiment of freedom on this noble planet. Human beings have always desired to be free and our souls are innately spiritual; so we pursue those things that will bring us spiritual growth, beauty, comfort, joy, peace, and happiness. We are adept at achieving material things, and can shape and reshape our world for our own pleasure, but now we have matured in our appreciation of what gives us true happiness. This human fulfillment is discovered through the exercise of ideas that will strengthen our soul's capacity and ability to achieve true freedom. Socrates described politics as the care of the soul. We can imagine the reaction today if a politician ran for office and said that his/her mission was to assist his/her constituents in setting the framework necessary for the care of our souls. However, that is precisely what we have joined together to do, today! As a nation, we have outgrown our youth and are now wiser and more mature, wanting to reclaim our heritage of freedom. Our birthright is one of individual freedom and our natural endowment is to live in a free nation. Our individual fulfillment is to be found not only in matter and in material objects but is also exercised through axiological ideas that will strengthen the soul's capacity for freedom — freedom of self, freedom of intellect, freedom of movement, and freedom of ratiocination. These fundamental expressions of liberty comprise the dimensions necessary for a freedom of self, i.e., the width, length, and height, or breadth of time and space that will emit the liberating energy that will transmute our material nation into a spiritual one: the heritage of the righteous and the birthright of our liberty. In the Age of Freedom, we are independent and emancipated, and utilize our knowledge gained from the sound ideas of past thinkers, who have nourished these concepts and independence. We ask ourselves what predominant ideas are the foundations for our free nation. Which idea should take precedent over another and which concepts advance our cause for freedom? Which one is true to our ideals, advancing our goal toward an expanded individual freedom for every citizen? What ideas stimulate our intellect and feed our souls? For guidance in our search for individual freedom, we seek Socrates whose dialectical exercise and vision will assist us in laying our own personal foundations. We boldly strike out with Socrates' guidance, and throw off the bounds of the known and seek paths that will lead us to new thoughts. Past thinkers can guide us; we follow a sound philosophy. If one person may be a guide by his virtue as a whole — and he is the one who spoke like a sage and strutted like a peacock, and gave us intellectual offspring in time — then we will follow Socrates.

The Socratic philosophy takes us out of our comfort zone, just as Socrates the philosopher took the ancient Athenians out of theirs. The exploration of any new philosophical territory is at the same time both exhilarating and uncomfortable. One can feel that he has been cast ashore onto a strange land, but a continued intellectual exploration of the new territory will reveal that what at first appeared to be very alien may in fact have some spatial aspects that are familiar to us. We can map the unfamiliar idea onto our logical thinking in order to stretch our imagination for philosophical discussion, examination, and reexamination leads to a dynamism that keeps philosophy alive. Our intellect and creative imaginative energy assists in carrying us forward to discover new ideas. Our character is innately a freedom-loving nature so our ideas will assist us in designing a model for this nation. For Socrates, man has an intrinsic sense of virtue and goodness that by necessity will be exercised by virtuous men and women, for they have an innate and rational sense of what is just, right, and good. Man is born free, but does not fully partake of this freedom until meditation upon the free self becomes coextensive with physical and material action within space and time. All formation and reformation in space is a canonical promotion of the free self, and what reclaims this free being is the activity of good citizens living within a good city.

Socrates taught individual autonomy and freedom in our own affairs. First, we seek to become a good person, and being a good citizen is the outcome of individual virtue. However, when the two conflict, as they did in His trial, he chooses moral freedom and autonomy. He had lived his life with these ethical principles and he would die upholding these ideas of goodness and justice. Man is born free and autonomous, but this freedom is recognized when his or her activities take place amongst other freedom-loving individuals. Socrates taught us that freedom becomes substantial and workable when it arises from within the receptacle of individuality, and only then is it exercised within the community. For Socrates, this meant that he energetically pursued his philosophical mission conversing with his fellow Athenians. However, in a city that valued democratic participation, he did not go into politics, claiming that his *daimonia* (his intuitive divine voice) warned him away from using his gifts as a politician.

Socrates did not consider himself a teacher, but he posed questions to numerous Athenians on a variety of topics. He was skilled in his *elenchus* where he used reasoning to guide the progress of the argument along with effective questions. Socrates personally took up the initiation of action in his dialectic for clarifying his preexisting mental experiments — what idea, concept, or experiment that he wanted to clarify for the sake of knowledge. Although we can never have a full understanding or knowledge of the Form of the Good, we are still guided by our beliefs about the good. Our proper rational activity will lead to the type of practical activity that determines a rational choice of the interests that serve the benefit of the whole soul.[84] When we study Socrates, we begin to understand that our personal freedom includes intellectual freedom, or freedom of our reasoning powers or ratiocination, and freedom of physical movements. Abstract thinking alone (although helpful in creative thinking) did not accomplish his goal of guiding his fellow Athenians to care for their souls. Socrates taught us that we can push an abstract thought to the extreme, and can abuse an abstraction, but until you try an idea against matter, we will not know whether it is a workable idea or not. Individual freedom is not just a theoretical construction or an abstract idea or concept, but is an active force when the replication of the ideas of the individual moving and living in space-time are constructed within.

The concept of freedom resonates in the intellect of each individual, and the principle of freedom is extended in a societal class. Each individual has a unique function in freedom, as does the community as a whole; they are similar in the end toward which they both seek, varying in degree but not in kind. This end is the maximum freedom for the individual living within a free community. To maintain our heritage of freedom and to achieve the end of the free community, our behavior will adhere to Socratic ethics, and collectively to an understanding of axiological ideas. An individual educated in philosophy is an individual animated in morality and spirit, and in turn, this person will assist in activating a good community. This moral, mental, and heartfelt concordance, as taught originally by Socrates, will nurture a future generation of gifted, free, and independent wisdom seekers, who will adhere to the precept that a community is activated through the spirit of freedom. Such a temporal community gives us a free scope in which we may correct past ideational errors and envision an enlightened future. The spatial configuration of such a community will matter in order that we can draft a design that will be in harmony with the figure of a moral philosophy, i.e. to architecturally mimic to the highest degree possible that which is beautiful and good in form and function. The citizens are the developers of this design and pattern and work together in order to bind the good city together. The citizens of this city have developed the best of natures, and are freedom loving and bearing individuals who are sound in mind, active in morality, and practicing in axiological ideas. For the individual living within a free community, freedom is superadded to existence even when the individual is passive in relationship to furthering the ends of freedom for the community; however, it is contiguous with existence when the individual is actively seeking its ideals.

As a nation, we express the good in form, i.e., in our Constitution, as an idea; the powers of government acquire a maximum force through the activity of good citizens not just through an idea. It is not only essential that the government, as the form of the community, allocates and distributes power as required by the law, but it is also necessary that the material, i.e., the citizens also fulfill their individual functions and their vocation as the electors of this representative democracy. The citizens are the ideational masters who feed the original form in order to enliven its function and capabilities, and this implies a strengthening (not an enlargement, as we have today) of the fundamental form. Our blessing as a nation is that we already possess a workable form in the Constitution, and the guardianship of government is the responsibility of each citizen, so that our protection and freedom under the Constitution for our rights, individually and collectively, does not degenerate into an autocratic regime. The value of the Constitution is increased when it engenders positive activity; the act of good citizenship can increase the value of the formal Constitution. The exercise of individual freedom — where citizens take an active role in society and government — adds to the development of the community and government as a whole. Many of the modern powers of the ruling body should be eliminated through individual citizen responsibility and administration. We are free to form a government, and we are at liberty to choose our leaders, therefore we need to dedicate ourselves to a lifetime study of the forms of good government and philosophy so that we may understand them, and recognize and support those who are capable of holding positions of leadership. The most expeditious way to clarify that which we already possess in form, and to restore our republican faith, is for a vigorous growth in the rise of new ideas and activity toward freedom. The intensification of spiritual energy — superadded to our everyday material for living well — will command an epoch of freedom, with creative and just individuals seeking to live happy lives within a community of free men and women.

As we follow the Socratic philosophy, we believe that freedom is an idea that will necessarily lead to action in order to keep the idea alive. Our intellect rests on a substructure of life: the freedom of the mind rests on a substructure of being; the freedom of the soul rests on a substructure of spirit, so the imperative maxim for a democratic community is that form which supports the foundation for individual freedom. The participators promote individualism, i.e., a dynamic process that is the stage for the direction of the energies of the individual. Freedom for the community is purchased through the aspiration of each individual's freedom of thought, for the conception of the community, as an isolated entity is false; it is an association of active individuals gaining momentum through education, practice, active participation and a robust exchange of ideas. The dignity of the citizen begins with his or her movement toward wisdom, a person who aspires toward wisdom is also an individual of action, and this action is always based upon spiritual health. If we take a foothold in our city from our own frame of reference, then we gain a confidence to participate in our community and our government. This interrelated security between the individual citizen, and their community and government is mutually beneficial because it affirms that we can acquire individual happiness and at the same time seek a stability of existence within. The problems that arise in a civilized society are solvable, and each solution leads to a further clarification of the magnitude of freedom, and a further specification of what it means to be free. Freedom evolves as we actively participate as citizens, and entails a vocation toward higher learning.

Our internal (or individual freedom) relates to the laws of the state, because it defines the boundaries of our external freedom. Government — without the individual freedom — will be a formless dictatorial entity. The foundation of our individual moral liberty is the root of our political liberty. A republican government will give us the amount of freedom that is equal to the capacitive freedom of the individuals in the state. As citizens seeking to form a good city, we establish the individual matrix of freedom that will translate to the creation of a liberated city. When we talk about this concept theoretically, the discussion will lead to action, where the unencumbered individual will translate his or her free mental accomplishments to the physical realm. Human association should be one of trust as the emancipation of the free individual reincarnates in a physical existence within the Free State. Our mission as philosophers, and lovers of Socrates and his wisdom, is to restore happiness, freedom, and fulfillment in a good city.

Freedom is the holy garment for a new intellect. Socrates' conceptual beliefs and philosophical wisdom gives us great insight for our growth as a species, for it is an innate and essential characteristic of the human being to be free. He taught that when in doubt, we should shun negativity and become a positive force, for when freedom is exercised, the human being discovers the true form of beauty, and its odorous sweetness awakens humankind to a spiritual reality in God.

CHAPTER EIGHT

The Nature of the Philosopher and the Good City

As philosophers, we do not seek to step outside of time, because everything of interest will occur in the here and now. As a child, do you remember your intense conception of time, where your imagination could transport you to another place, another country, or a different era? Children have very active temporal sensations — their sensory apparatus, including the perception of color are very finely tuned. If an innocent child were to sit across from us today and point to a pure color, we would be unable to see it, for the sensation would be so overwhelming, as to cause pain. Children live in earnest activity; however, as adults, we tend to lose that same degree of focus, and intensity. What ideas could we derive if we were more earnest and resolute? Therefore, let us re-focus our thoughts, open our creative minds, and return to simple, pure concepts as we explore philosophy together.

The Republic, written by Plato approximately 380 B.C., defines justice, the just man, and the character of a just city-state. Socrates and his fellow Athenians discuss the meaning of justice, a city ruled by philosopher-kings, the theory of forms, and the immortality of the soul. As we learn philosophical truths, each aspect of the good city becomes more vivid, and the whole archetype becomes a pattern for it. Our activity needed to create this city is the spiritual energy from the well of truth. Solving problems from past writers who have written about this concept is also helpful.85 It is a wonderful adventure as we set out together as the creators of a good community, where the quality of life for each citizen will surpass the good works that each member will achieve through his natural powers. Each member is remarkable in his or her constitution, yet more extraordinary is the composition of the entire city. We have all experienced our share of sorrows in life, and have prayed when we hear of the misfortune that befalls upon others, and we witness evil acts that seem to be more prevalent today than in the past. We are all in the world together struggling toward the light, appearing to make progress, and then suffering setbacks. Fortune will feed each individual as we are nursed back to our spiritual health within a good community. Situated within our framework within the United States it is important to seek the application of what we have learned through our inductive study of Socrates. Our fulfillment is to be found in matter and material objects and is exercised through spiritual activity that will strengthen the soul's capacity for freedom.

Our good city is within a nation where human beings are free to worship a holy God.

We search for the apple-hung branch, but what price will we pay for admittance into that sacred orchard? We are the heirs of the Ancient Greek mythology, and these ancient myths are deeply embedded in our psyche and part of our metaphysical nature. Through a Socratic study, we gain an intuitive separation between myths and concrete ideas, and we awaken from our primitive slumber. The manifestation of our power is found in the idea of individual freedom. Socrates, I am certain, would tell us modern citizens that knowledge without intellect is brute force that will create a human incapable of feeling and heart-felt development of spirit. The exercise of our spiritual nature takes place within the finite form of individual freedom, and reveals itself as the movement of a free being in time, but this must begin with a developed spirit. Socratic virtue is a unity of all the virtues in one, that is, in knowledge. Our heritage as Americans is to be blessed with the exterior form of freedom in democracy, and now we must seize this as part of our entitative being, therefore, strengthening all forms of exterior freedom. We demonstrate resoluteness toward freedom when we consider what we have inherited is also, what we would have chosen. The desire for an individual freedom is our yearning to be a whole spiritual person, and will set the pattern for an aesthetic enjoyment of life, and a clearer and intuitive understanding of what it means to be free. Socrates stands forever at the pinnacle of this knowledge because he taught us how to look inward while at the same time looking outward, and this absorption and reabsorption is the beginning of individual freedom.

We are like the ancient students of Athens — we go beyond history to understand the historical, and we go beyond philosophy to understand the philosophical concept of freedom. There have been many famous philosophers, but never one like Socrates, who labored steadily for the improvement of the Athenian soul. If our spirit resides with him what are our current thoughts for a materialistic America, whose citizens would — if they discovered a modern Socrates rambling about the marketplace and disturbing their ideas — vote a fate for him no better than the ancients would? America may not be ready for him, but she is equipped for the true meaning of individual freedom, i.e., one that begins with an idea, but ends with function. We will utilize our ideas of individual freedom to better our souls, and then to build a better community for our families and ourselves. Individual freedom is both a humanistic project and a transcendental concept: a humanistic one because it is the practice of living a worthy life, and a transcendental concept because it is the vital form, which gives value to a developing and active soul. Socrates taught us that freedom without goodness is amoral and freedom as power is immoral.

He demonstrated that a citizen of a good city is imbued with the spirit and soul of virtue. Our goal is to take our loftiest achievement, democracy, and introduce the idea of an individual citizen imbued with the spirit and soul of virtue. Individual freedom is related to knowledge, action, and subsequent freedom — the concept is a temporal-spatial one and is important for the individual growth of the human being.

What is a natural political system for humankind? When we think of anything as natural, we conceive of it as being in its original form. In addition, when we think of a political system we think of it as being a generated governmental power. Let us, philosophically define natural as that element which is essential to a particular thing and politics as that entity which is structured for the maximum amount of good for the community. Socrates taught us that there can be no philosophers without the wisdom of philosophy; and there can be no politics without the understanding of what is good. As human beings and truth-seekers, our association in a good community is for the benefit of each member, and is obtained through the political matrix that seeks out the maximum amount of good, essential for the maintenance of the city.

CHAPTER NINE

Passing of Night's Scepter to Day's Crown

"God so loved the world that he gave us the treasure of His Holy Son to be sacrificed on the cross so that we may not perish but have everlasting life" (John 3:16). Jesus gathers His students around Him so that we may learn more about Him and therein deepen our love and understanding for the Lord. "Thou shall love the Lord thy God with all thy heart." The inductive methodology that Socrates used so successfully is the method that assists us in understanding the Bible with the goal of increasing our intimacy with the Word of God so that we may have a personal relationship with Him. In logic, we infer conclusions or principles from facts or specifics in order to come to logical conclusions. Inductive reasoning is reasoning that derives general principles from specific observations or specific concepts. Another definition of induction is reasoning from the particular cases to the general idea or concept. The practice of inductive reasoning is an important tool for understanding and learning the Bible. For our Biblical studies, inductive methodology means that we will interpret the scripture without bringing our own pre-judgments or preconceived views to the interpretation. Socrates used induction in his cross-examination where he would have his subject set aside his or her prejudice in order to gain a clearer understanding of a concept or the topic under discussion. The interpretation and meaning of the Bible belongs to God as His Holy Word, so with the spirit of humility, as children of God, we come to the classroom to receive our Father's teaching, not to invent our own. God uses repeated examples to teach His servants, so it is by our critical reading — and our power of observation — that we come to sound conclusions about the meaning of the Bible. Our interpretation is from specific and consistent text: the scripture is the source, and its books are harmonious and the whole is inerrant. For example, Christ taught us about God and God's love for us by detailing His Holy attributes and thereby revealing His Holy Father. The Bible gives us an account of the life, death, resurrection, and ascension of Jesus the Messiah. This inductive thesis encourages the reader to discover the Holy Word and to continue the message of Jesus, and to unfold the message of salvation from Jerusalem to the ends of the earth. The age of salvation has arrived in Jesus Christ and the Holy Spirit as taught to us through His ministry. We pray that modern Christian believers will grow in their faith by reading and studying The Sacred transcripts, and that the utilization of inductive methodology — our gifts from Socrates and our heritage from Christ — will provide some additional understanding of the Holy Word.

We will discuss the techniques and principles of inductive study after we discuss a brief history of the theory. We will place inductive reasoning in an historical context, which will help us to understand the methodology that we will be implementing. No mind, other than the superior mind of our Lord, has so profoundly utilized induction for guidance and growth other than Socrates, through the voice of Plato. Our intent in moving from the secular to the sacred is to sharpen our observation so that we may correctly study, interpret, and understand the Bible. To observe well is to interpret well; our goal is to apply God's truth in our Christian lives. Interpretation is defined as the art of explaining or telling the meaning of something and presenting it in understandable terms. For example, we can interpret God's truth as God lovingly offers us absolute truth. The Platonic skills of Socrates can assist us in sharpening our tools for hermeneutics —the science and art of interpretation — and a brief presentation of the philosopher Socrates' inductive teaching will assist us in understanding inductive methodology with the goal of understanding God's profound truths.

When we practice Socratic philosophy, we note all of the relevant distinctions, similarities, agreements, contrasts, divisions, and ambiguities in ideas and the terms. This critical methodology opens the intellectual horizons for a wider inquiry into the nature of things. Our search — in both the mundane and sacred realms — is the search for correct concepts, whereby everything (the particulars) will radiate from its general conception, and then we can judge the truth of things. We seek out symbols and learn from them: from the Platonic Cave to Socrates' meaning of that which is Good, and the Socratic daimonion (or spiritual guide who helped Socrates live his life); our mundane knowledge increases with the aid of symbols. As children of God, we also seek out sacred symbols in the Holy Bible: from Moses and the pillars of fire guiding the Israelites, from the Ark of the Holy Covenant, Noah's Ark, the Angelic Messengers of God, the Holy Cross, and the "unleashed Holy Spirit" in Acts — we are divinely guided by representations. Our intimacy with our Holy God is illuminated and strengthened with these aids and the symbolic truth is our holy guidance from God, as the Absolute Truth emanates from Him. Contrast the analogy of Plato's Cave; the symbolic truth leads us in the mundane realm, step by step, to the absolute truth of the Platonic Good. Our inductive study of the Bible and the symbolic truths of the Lord will lead us, in the sacred realm, gradually, to the absolute truths of God. His symbols remain sealed until we have the eyes to see and the mature intellect to understand them. Just as the Bible reveals more meaning to us as we grow and mature in our intimacy and love for God, our divine schooling is a stage-by-stage learning that brings us joyfully to the knowledge of our destiny in the Lord. We pray to God; enter his pure child to direct and enlighten us to the true meaning of the holy symbols. The profound philosophy of the adult falls away to nothingness as a sealed mind and heart unseals itself in the growth of God's divine child.

Plato's pattern of thinking — where he looked beyond particulars in the immediate world to the universals that were real — had a profound influence on Christians who later had to develop deep religious thinking about their beliefs and faith in the resurrected Jesus Christ. The Hellenistic Greek philosophy and dialectic of ideas influenced the voice embodied in the believers of the Christian message, where the whole act of speech or the idea or thought behind the speech then flows into conversation, narrative, reason, dialogue, and oral religious teaching. Historically, the allegorical method (also used by Socrates) was utilized by the Early Church Fathers until the time of Origin (ca. 185-254 A.D.), where one looks for hidden meaning, rather than accepting the plain meaning of the text. Augustine was influential in attempting to harmonize Platonic philosophy and Scripture. This is not my goal. Scripture and the Word of God are sacred; Platonic philosophy is secular, and the voice of Socrates is one of wisdom but it is an earthly proclamation. The point that I am making is that we can benefit from the philosophical and intellectual tools provided to us by Plato, that is, inductive reasoning, dialectic, and the understanding of symbols, concepts, and ideas to enlarge our minds with the principles of logic and communication. These tools can only benefit us in our Bible study; God is not the Author of confusion, but is the Author of clarity and His truth.

We can understand the profound and spiritual side of our nature when abstractions are presented to us with allegoric examples and stories, for example, parables that Jesus Christ uses to teach us. Our exile from heaven is painful to our soul, so all of the methods that the ancient Greeks used — inductive and deductive reasoning, logic, allegories, dialectic, and stories — are helpful in moving us, God's creatures back to our spiritual home. Socrates wanted to "sting us out of our forgetfulness", and Christ's mission was to give us salvation and awaken us to the power of the Holy Spirit. As our Christian belief is strengthened in our secular space, we become more deeply rooted in our heavenly sacred universe. To leave a legacy of our beliefs, then we must embrace these heavenly gifts and allow God to transform these into something of prominence for His glory and purpose.

An additional guide in our inductive study is from the seminal work *Living by the Book: The Art and Science of Reading the Bible,* by Howard G. Hendricks.[86] We learn to follow in the Lord's steps when we read the Holy Bible. We are called to be disciples of Jesus so we are pupils or learners of the Holy Word. God commands us to study the Scriptures and to know God's Word (Josh 1:8, Jer 23:28-29, Psalms 119:9-11, Acts 17:11, Tim 2:14-16, Heb 4:12). The inductive study method is the most valuable and accurate way of studying the scriptures. This method focuses on three main areas of study: context, historical background, and language, and should be examined and always kept in mind. The first step is observation; the second — interpretation and the third is the application. Dr Howard Hendricks's book *Living by the Book* adds a fourth step — correlation or communication. Our Christian study of the Bible is not an option, it is essential to Christian growth (1 Pet 2:2). We must maintain a certain rigorousness to our study and observation in order to achieve sound results. We open our mind and heart to the Holy Spirit via our prayers for understanding the Holy Word, and through Christian-to-Christian communication which enables us to joyfully share what we learn.

When we utilize the inductive methodology to study our Bible, the parts take on meaning in light of the whole. We observe and then we ask, what does it say? We learn to ask the right questions, and God will reveal the answers. When we read and study the Bible, we learn to follow in the Lord's steps. Prior to communing with the Lord in His Word is prayer, where we ask the Lord for guidance in our understanding and to be in His light and Word. In the first step, we record the obvious observations, i.e., what we are being told in the text of the Bible, for example, sanctification, prayer, the Holy Spirit, and love. It is helpful if we record the natural division in each section of the chapters, or the entire book. Good observation will lead to accurate interpretation. We should always read (and re-read) the text in order to judge what the Word is saying to us and in turn, this will enable us to think for ourselves, and to fall in love with God and His Word. Dr Hendricks suggests that we may consult commentaries to compare our thinking with the thinking of others, but first we should read the text, to come to a better understanding. Bible concordances, lexicons, dictionaries, encyclopedias, word studies, language studies, commentaries, maps, and computer research are all useful tools after we have perused the Holy Book.

The second step is the interpretation that focuses on the hermeneutics, context, history, language, and discovering what these mean to us. Researching the historical background will assist us with the interpretation of the text. Be aware of the original language — Hebrew, Aramaic, or Greek, however, being proficient with them is not a necessity, for there are excellent translations of key terms available that can shed light on your subject matter. Remember that our goal is transformation, not information (2 Cor 5:17). An outline of the chapter or book can show the relationships of the major and minor points. List the key words and terms that appear to be emphasized or focused in the verse or chapter. List key phrases that are repeated or emphasized, and observe that each verse or chapter will have a key verse or verses. Identify the theological themes in each section, and passage, or identify the theme of the whole book, and note how the themes relate to each other. Always keep in mind the inductive questions: who, what, where, when, why and how. What do I see? Who is involved and what do they say, and what do you know about them from your previous Bible study? What is happening and where did it occur? At this point, it is helpful to refer to a map of the ancient world so that we can become familiar with where the action is taking place. What reason is the particular action occurring? Why did God indicate this in the Bible? Was it to build belief, or faith in the Son of God? Observe what preceded the event described, and what follows the event in the Bible. How does this apply to me? Is it a lesson that we can in turn speak to within the needs of others? The

Scripture itself will clarify, support, supplement, complement, and interpret the Holy Word for us. The Holy Spirit will illuminate your spiritual mind as you prayerfully study the Holy Bible. "Now we have received, not the spirit of the world, but the Spirit who is from God, so that we may know the things freely given to us by God, which things we also speak, not in words taught by human wisdom, but in those taught by the Spirit, combining spiritual thoughts with spiritual words" (1 Cor 2:12-13).

The interpretation of your observation is very important, i.e., what does it mean to me? Dr Hendricks provides five keys to interpret: 1) content 2) context 3) comparison 4) culture 5) consultation. Knowledge of the content is the fruit of our observation. We begin by examining the content through the process of observation: look for contrasts, cause and effect, questions and answers, and repetition. A thorough reading of the passage, a knowledgeable perspective, and meditation are helpful for your observation and understanding. The context means understanding what happened before and after — both will give meaning to the current text that you are studying. Comparison with other scriptures is also a key element in your accurate interpretation and a Bible concordance will assist you with this project. An understanding of the culture is important because it will enlighten you as to why certain practices were implemented, e.g., in ancient cultures the washing of feet was performed to remove the dust and dirt from a traveler. In conclusion, it is helpful to consult other resources and Dr Hendricks reminds us that these resources can help put you back on track, if your personal interpretation has deluded you.

The third step is the application that centers on the practical and relevant truth to be lived as a Christian. How does it apply to me in daily living! We are taught regeneration, sanctification, illumination, and glorification through the Holy Word. Is our belief in Jesus Christ practiced in trust, obedience to the Word, prayer, reading, involvement in the church, exercising the gifts of the Spirit, and in sharing the gospel with unbelievers?

If we know the truth, how do we relate to it? "Therefore if anyone is in Christ, he is a new creature; the old things pass away; behold, new things have come" (2 Cor 5:17). The application is built on the interpretation; and if the interpretation is wrong, then the application will be in error. Your work is your ministry and you want this based on a solid foundation of truth. Meditate on the scriptures day and night so that the light of their purpose takes meaning in your everyday journey. "This book of the law shall not depart from your mouth, but you shall meditate on it day and night, so that you may be careful to do according to all that is written in it; for then you will make your way prosperous, and then you will have success" (Joshua 1:8). Pray and ask that God will use your light and relate the truth of the Lord to the Light in the world and society. "With all my heart I have sought You; Do not let me wander from Your commandments" (Psalms 119:10). Ask yourself how does it work, is there an example to follow, is there a sin to avoid, is there a promise to claim, and is there a prayer to repeat? Apostle Paul taught, "Therefore I, the prisoner of the Lord, implore you to walk in a manner worthy of the calling with which you have been called, with all humility and gentleness, with patience, showing tolerance for one another in love being diligent to preserve the unity of the Spirit in the bond of peace. There is one body and one Spirit; just as also you were called in one hope of your calling; one Lord, one faith, one baptism, one God and Father of all who is over all and through all and in all. But to each one of us grace was given according to the measure of Christ's gift" (Eph 4:1-7). We read the Bible and consciously seek the law of God, but our humble preparation in the Lord must be followed by active Christian practices. Do we live, practice, preach, and teach God's law? The study of the Bible transforms our life into the model human being that Christ taught us to be. We pray for discipline, habit, sanctification, and eternal life in the Lord.

There are different styles of Scripture, all from the Word of God, but an identification of the style or form will help in the interpretation of the Scripture. Six major literary genres are used in the Bible to communicate His message to us: exposition, narrative and biography, parables, poetry, the proverbs and wisdom literature, and prophecy and apocalyptic. We also add a seventh category to these six, i.e., didactic or teaching, and an example is found in the book of Romans. Exposition is a carefully reasoned argument or explanation that is also well organized and logical. The goal is agreement and action: examples are Paul's letters, Hebrews, James, 1 and 2 Peter, and John. Paul teaches, "But now Christ has been raised from the dead, the first fruits of those who are asleep. For since by a man came death, by a man also came the resurrection of the dead. For as in Adam all die, so also in Christ all will be made alive. But each in his own order: Christ the first fruits, after that those who are Christ's at His coming, then comes the end, when He hands over the kingdom to the God and Father, when He has abolished all rule and all authority and power: For He must reign until He has put all His enemies under His feet. The last enemy that will be abolished is death" (1 Cor 15:20-26).

The narrative is where the story is prominent and includes historical accounts, a plot structure, characters that undergo psychological and spiritual development and events that convey contrast, comparison, and meaning. The biography is the close up of an individual's life, an eyewitness account of events, and characters that may develop in a positive or negative manner. Examples of narrative are Genesis through the book of Ezra, the Gospels, and Acts; and examples of biography are the stories of Abraham, Isaac, Joseph, Moses, Saul, David, Elijah, and Jesus. God tested Abraham and told him to take his son and offer him as a burnt offering, "Then they came to the place of which God had told him; and Abraham built the altar there and arranged the wood, and bound his son Isaac and laid him on the altar, on top of the wood. Abraham stretched out his hand and took the knife to slay his son. But the angel of the Lord called to him from heaven and said, 'Abraham, Abraham!' And he said, 'Here I am.' He said, 'Do not stretch out your hand against the lad, and do nothing to him; for I know that you fear God, since you have not withheld your son, your only son, from Me.' Then Abraham raised his eyes and looked, and behold, behind him a ram caught in the thicket by his horns; and Abraham went and took the ram and offered him up for a burnt offering in the place of his son" (Gn 22:9-13).

The Biblical parables offer brief stories that illustrate morals, truth, reflection, and self-evaluation. We find parables in the Gospels of Mathew, Mark and Luke, and one parable, the sheep gate, and the shepherd in John (John 10:7-16). Jesus taught us in forty-six parables, "Therefore I speak to them in parables; because while seeing they do not see, and while hearing they do not hear nor do they understand" (Mat 13:13). Jesus shares this allegory in the gospel of Luke, "And he began telling this parable: A man had a fig tree which had been planted in his vineyard; and he came looking for fruit on it and did not find any. And he said to the vineyard-keeper, 'Behold, for three years I have come looking for fruit without finding any. Cut it down! Why does it even use up the ground?' And he answered and said to him, 'Let it alone, sir, for this year too, until I dig it and put in fertilizer; and if it bears fruit next year, fine; but if not, cut it down' " (Luke 13:6-9).

Poetry in the Bible was meant to be spoken or sung rather than read, and we find an emphasis on the sound of the words, vivid images, and symbols with an appeal to the emotions. We find poetry in Job, Psalms, Proverbs, Ecclesiastes, and the Song of Solomon. "The Mighty One, God, the Lord, has spoken, And summoned the earth from the rising of the sun to its setting. Out of Zion, the perfection of beauty, God has shone forth. May our God come and not keep silence; Fire devours before Him. He summons the heavens above, And the earth, to judge His people: 'Gather My godly ones to Me, Those who have made a covenant with me by sacrifice.' And the heavens declare His righteousness, For God Himself is judge" (Psalms 50:1-6).

The Proverbs are short pithy statements of a moral truth, and direct the reader toward what is right and away from evil, uses similes and metaphors, and reduces life to simple terms in order to make a moral point. We locate these adages in the book of Proverbs. Wisdom literature is when an older person relates wisdom to a younger person on birth, life, death, work, money, power, time, and human experience. These works can be found in Job, Proverbs, Psalms 37 and 90, and Ecclesiastes. "Better is the little of the righteous Than the abundance of many wicked" (Prov 37:16).

Didactic or teaching in the Bible can be found in Romans where Paul teaches us that we, both Jew and Gentile, are only acceptable to God through the New Covenant in Christ who is the propitiation for our sin. In Romans 5, Adam is contrasted with Christ: Adam is the human being who stands at the beginning, whose action determined the fate of humanity; but Christ stands at the beginning of a new humanity, whose actions are determined by those who follow Him.

Prophecy and apocalyptic genre are found, respectively, in Isaiah through Malachi, and in Revelation. Prophecy is authoritative presentation of God's will and intended to motivate change through warnings. Revelation is the dramatic and symbolic events that take place on a global scale and portrays a cosmic struggle between good and evil. Revelation is understood through a corresponding study of the Book of Daniel, Christian ministers, teachers, authors, commentaries, and the enlightenment of the Holy Spirit. Read and study God's Holy Word first and then consult your Biblical resources. The Apostle John wrote, "Then I saw a new heaven and a new earth; for the first heaven and the first earth passed away, and there is no longer any sea. And I saw the holy city, New Jerusalem, coming down out of heaven from God, made ready as a bride adorned for her husband. And I heard a loud voice from the throne, saying, 'Behold the tabernacle of God is among men, and he will dwell among them, and they shall be His people, and God himself will be among them, and He will wipe away every tear from their eyes; and there will no longer be any death; there will no longer be any mourning, or crying, or pain; the first things have passed away.' And He who sits on the throne said, 'Behold, I am making all things new.' And He said, 'Write, for these words are faithful and true' " (Rev 21:1-5).

To summarize the inductive methodology that this author recommends for the study of the Bible (and first taught to us by Socrates), we reason from specific to general propositions. Socrates taught us how to ascribe properties or a relationship to types that was based on limited observations of particular tokens, or objects. Inductive reasoning can also formulate principles based on limited observation of recurring phenomenal patterns. Questions that assist us both in studying Platonic philosophy, and in studying the Holy Bible are a) What is the chapter about? b) Who are the main characters? c) When does this event or teaching take place? d) Where does this happen? e) Why is this being done or said? f) How did it happen? g) How is it symbolic? God teaches us through holy symbols so that we may learn of His love for us; however, God's representations remain sealed until we have His Spirit within us to enable us to understand His mystery and love. God may also shift His symbols to guide us closer to His love. We asked all of these questions during our inductive study of Socratic philosophy. We also ask all of these questions during our inductive study of the Bible to assist us to see, observe, and understand what the Word of God is saying, and to be filled with the Holy Spirit, His appointed teacher. The time element is also very important in our growth as human beings, and we ask when is the event taking place, and how does it relate to our development as Christians? Our concept of ourselves as followers of Christ are assessed over time and the experience must be repeated over and over again so that we may bear witness to the truth of the Christian principles of 'self'. There is a holy bond between freedom in Christ and reality, and this holy bond is exercised in time. There is also a spatial element to our growth, and we ask how people, places, and things relate to one another in the cosmos. The virtuous Christian establishes a viable blueprint for direction, as we grow as spiritual beings; therefore, we will utilize our inductive methodology to discern our biblical lessons towards this goal.

The Lord presents us with the Holy Word and His teaching remains holy, precise and without any contradictions. When the Lord teaches us, for example, to be transformed (John 13:21), be alive (John 1:12), be courageous (Luke 14:24), and be compassionate (Luke 1:130), these are characteristics that a Christian will earnestly develop. However, while we are studying and practicing — these positive virtues, symbols and concepts from our secular instruction will come to mind to assist us in our understanding of what is required of us in the sacred realm. As children of God, the Bible teaches us to be divinely guided by symbols: the burning bush, the Holy Ark of the Covenant, God's pillar of fire, the rainbow, the dove, the eagle, the vine, bread and wine, the door, His cross, His grave, and His throne. When we encounter these divine symbols we immediately have an image of a mundane object in the secular realm, and the guidance of the symbolic truth of the symbol leads us, step by step, to the absolute truth of the sacred realm: God's Truth. His divine alphabet is contained within these Biblical symbols, so sacred and profound that their meaning remains obscure to us until God's child enters as our instructor to teach us the meaning of the holy symbols.

As Christians, we seek God's truth, and many of His truths remain sealed to us until we have the eyes to see, the ears to hear, and the maturity to understand. As we study to show ourselves approved before our Lord, the Holy Spirit can open God's Word to us. There are symbols in the secular realm that God uses to guide us on our journey to Him. (Plato was a master in the use of symbols; see for example, the Allegory of the Cave, and the Divided Line.) There are also symbols that the devil and the kingdom of evil uses, so we must learn and practice discernment to stay in the light. When a person is in Jesus Christ, he will see everything in the world as symbols of the Lord's Sovereign Being and holy activity. Things in the world will make sense in a very new way. When we think of the changes brought about when Jesus taught and the pre-existing notions of the historic Messiah replaced with the Truth — we thank the Lord for the pure and childlike glimpses of our life to be!

The prophets of ancient Israel talked about a fundamental transformation of human nature, by following God from the Exodus under Moses, to the Monarchy under Saul (1445 B.C. to 1051 B.C.). Centuries after Moses, the philosophy of Plato and Socrates postulated the possibility of the transformation of human nature by following moral and ethical duties. Socrates' moralizing manifested itself when he prompted everyone — both young and old, shoemakers, blacksmiths, politicians, playwrights, Sophists, and citizens of every stratum — to think about their duties.

Ancient Jewish thought did not speculate into the nature of God, but was interested in man's duties to Him and one another. God has a personal relationship with His creatures while at the same time remaining beyond characterization. His is the voice that tells Moses out of the burning bush, "I AM WHO I AM" (Ex 3:14). The One True Lord of the Israelites replaced the pantheon of gods, whose jealousies guarded ceremonial observances. Even the golden age of the Greeks in the 6th century B.C. is resplendent with temples and centers of worship for sacrifices in order to perpetuate the gods' favor on the populace. Socrates battled dead religion and gave us a moral compass for our individual actions, and improving our souls. Our Lord Jesus Christ battled dead religion and gave us the promise of an eternal life; He is the Victor in His death on the cross and His Resurrection. His victory is our salvation.

CHAPTER TEN

Genesis: Intimate with God

The God of Genesis is not one of the limited and localized gods of the ancient civilizations who were worshipped through idolatry, superstitious practices, sacrifices and appeasement. We ache for an intimacy with God, although His sublime and sweet mystery is beyond our comprehension. He has provided us with a classroom — and the inductive tools of methodology — for us to decipher how things run (although His sacred Creation remains a blessed mystery to us!). When we ask why we are addressing Moses in our book about Socrates and Jesus, the answer is that our application of this knowledge is to worship and obey God and open our hearts to His Holiness so that we may grow in the Lord. In order to practice our inductive methodology, we move backward in time in order to progress forward as creatures of His light. The inductive question 'what' is demonstrated when we encounter the God of Genesis who is an all-powerful, almighty Creator who created and loves humankind, cares for them, and judges their misdeeds. Genesis relates stories and events, and when we ask ourselves the question 'why' we study these actions, it is because they disclose the nature of God and His purposes. These chapters are the book of origins, source, and creation, "In the beginning God created the heavens and the earth" (Gn 1:1). Genesis is a history of beginnings, births, genealogies, and generations, and a narrative that includes historical accounts, a structure that is conveyed through the plot, and characters that undergo psychological and spiritual development. When we ask our inductive 'when' and 'who' questions, we discover that Genesis was written by Moses approximately 1440 B.C. It is the first book of the Pentateuch (the first five books of the Bible, also called "the Law"). When we ask our 'why' question we learn that the book was written to record God's creation of the world and to demonstrate His love for all that He created. We ask our 'what' and 'who' questions, and learn that Genesis describes the Lord God, who is infinite and all-powerful, and created matter out of nonmaterial nothing. We add an additional time element to our induction and observe that it spans more time than any other book in the Bible: from the time of creation and Adam, to the time of Joseph when the Israelites arrived in Egypt and grew into a nation (approximately 1800 B.C.).

"Then God said, 'Let us make man in Our image, according to Our likeness; and let them rule over the fish of the sea and over the birds of the sky and over the cattle and over all the earth, and over every creeping thing that creeps on the earth' " (Gn 1:26). "God created man in His own image, in the image of God He created him;

male and female he created them" (Gn 1:27). When we read the key word 'created', we understand that Adam and Eve had every need provided for them by God in the Garden of Eden. Adam and Eve were without flaw; they were spiritually and physically perfect in body, soul, and spirit. When we read the key word 'seed' we interpret and understand God's spiritual law and every living thing produces after its own kind: humans produce humans and animals produce animals. On the day that God created humankind He planted a seed of His nature into our human spirit, so that His life and nature would be reproduced and grow. "Out of the ground the Lord God caused to grow every tree that is pleasing to the sight and good for food; the tree of life also in the midst of the garden, and the tree of the knowledge of good and evil" (Gn 2:9). "The Lord commanded the man, saying, 'From any tree of the garden you may eat freely; but from the tree of the knowledge of good and evil you shall not eat, for in that day that you eat from it you will surely die' " (Gn 1:16-17). The question of 'what happened' is answered when we learn that Satan tempted Eve and she ate of the forbidden fruit, and then she gave the forbidden fruit to Adam to eat. Adam blamed Eve, and Eve blamed the serpent. The fall dramatically altered the nature of humankind. Adam and Eve, who had been created perfect and communed with God in the Garden of Eden, were now darkened in sin, and spiritually dead after the fall. They were no longer able to commune with God, and they were not able to understand the things that come from His Spirit. When we meditate on the spatial aspect of the story, we induce that His once perfect creation became corrupt, and sin and death entered into time and space. We observe that His new creation willingly chose to sin and that Adam and Eve lost their position and dominion over the earth. We apply the creation story to our own lives; we know by failure our own weaknesses, and we voluntarily choose God. We are all His children but Satan who became the "prince of this world" is at work against those who are obedient to God's Word.

Genesis is full of instructions for the Christian: in this book, we read about the origin of the universe with the creation (Gn 1:1-2). The fall (Gn 3), the flood (Gn 6-9), the confusion of tongues (Gn 11), the destruction of Sodom and Gomorrah from fire from the Lord out of heaven (Gn 19), the sacrifice of Isaac (Gn 28:10-22), Jacob cheats Esau of his blessing (Gn 26:34-29:9), Jacob meets God at Bethel (Gn 28:10-22), Joseph's brothers sell him into Egypt (Gn 37:2-36), Joseph in Potiphar's house, Joseph in prison (Gn 39:1-23; 40:1-23), Joseph interprets Pharaoh's dreams (Gn 41:1-39), and Pharaoh gave Joseph power and command over all of the land of Egypt because of Joseph's wisdom (Gn 41:41-57). Genesis is the story of the birth of the Hebrew nation, and the four great God-fearing men: Abraham, Isaac, Jacob, and Joseph. As well as the key words: begat, seed, generation, and begin, we would like to add the key word "blessings". God created us for blessings and chose us to be a blessing to the world and to others. It is through one faithful man, Abraham, that God calls and promises to bless them with a multitude of people, and through them bless the entire world. The Lord told Abraham to "go forth from your country, and from your relatives and from your father's house, to the land which I will show you; and I will make you a great nation, and I will bless you and make your name great; and so you shall be a blessing; and I will bless those who bless you, and the one who curses you, I will curse. And in you all families of the earth shall be blessed" (Gn 12:1-3). God faithfully rises up and protects the generations from Abraham as He had promised. Abraham fell on his face when God spoke to him saying, "My covenant is with you, And you will be the father of a multitude of nations" (Gn 17:4). God blesses Abraham's sons and their sons, and He displays His power and sovereignty in their lives even when they have disappointments and failures. Our interpretation of the stories in Genesis is that every condition of failure by humankind is met by the salvation of God.

Genesis does span space and time — and is quoted from over two hundred times in the New Testament demonstrating that the New Testament is the written Word of the fulfillment of God's promise to us in the Old Testament: He will send a savior, our Lord Jesus Christ, to bring deliverance from servitude to sin and Satan. God chose the Hebrew nation as the people from whom the Redeemer would come. We inductively learn about our Lord from the specific Messianic prophecies: Christ is the Seed of woman (Gn 3:15), from the line of Seth (Gn 4:25), the son of Shem (Gn 9:27), the descendent of Abraham (Gn 12:3), of Isaac (Gn 21:12), of Jacob (Gn 25:23), and of the tribe of Judah (Gn 49:10). Christ is also seen in people and events that serve as types (a "type" is a historical fact that illustrates a spiritual truth). Adam is the head of the old creation; and Christ is the Head of God's new creation. Both Adam and Christ entered the world through a special act of God as sinless men. Both Joseph and Christ are objects of special love by their Fathers, both are hated by their brethren, and both are rejected as rulers. Both are conspired against and sold for silver, are condemned though innocent, and then are raised from humiliation to glory by the power of God. Christ is the King of Peace who brings forth bread and wine and is the priest of the Most High God. Our application is the knowledge that the sin of man is met by the intervention and redemption of God. He created us for blessings and chose us as a blessing to the world, and to others.

In the end of Genesis, God's chosen people are in a foreign locale and are wondering about the Promised Land. Jacob becomes ill, so he gathers Joseph and Joseph's sons about him and said, "Behold, I am about to die, but God be with you, and bring you back to the land of your fathers" (Gn 48:21). Jacob then assembles his own sons and blesses each of them, and tells them what will befall them in the days ahead (Gn 49). 'Blessing' was one of the key words in Genesis, and Jacob's blessings to his sons include abundant water supplies (rain), springs, many children, and fertile hilltops. From the culture and customs, we can deduce from the biblical fact that when Jacob died he was embalmed, therefore, he held a high status in Egypt (Gn 50:3). The funeral procession was "a very great company" (Gn 50:9), and they passed by "the threshing-floor of Atad" (Gn 50:11), which indicates that it was somewhere near Gaza or Jericho, and implies that the funeral procession took a similar route to the Israelites in the exodus. When Jacob died, "his sons carried him to the land of Canaan and buried him in the cave of the field of Machpelah before Mamre, which Abraham had bought — along with the field for a burial site — from Ephrom the Hittite" (Gn 50:13). The 'where' i.e., the location of the funeral procession and the burial are important not only for the fact that the sons are carrying out their father's last wishes, but it is an act on the prophecy of the exodus, when all of Jacob's descendants would leave Egypt and return to the promised land. After Jacob's death, Joseph forgives his brothers for their transgressions, "you meant evil against me, but God meant it for good in order to bring about this present result, to preserve many people alive" (Gn 50:20). Before Joseph dies, he tells his brothers that God would lead his people back to the Promised Land and he also requests, "you shall carry my bones up from here" (Gn 50:25).

Genesis is the river of truth that runs throughout the Bible and flows into the Book of Revelation. Jesus referred to the creation of Adam and Eve, to the flood, and to the destruction of Sodom and Gomorrah. He even referred to Satan as a murderer from the beginning. Jesus affirmed the teachings of Genesis and the Holy Bible. He said to them, "Truly, truly, I say to you, before Abraham was born, I am" (John 8:58). Jesus said to them, "These are My words which I spoke to you while I was still with you, that all things which are written about Me in the Laws of Moses and the Prophets and the Psalms must be fulfilled" (Luke 24:44). "In the beginning was the Word, and the Word was with God, and the Word was God" (John 1:1). "And the Word became flesh, and dwelt among us, and we saw His glory, glory as of the only begotten from the Father, full of grace and truth" (John 1:14).

"For the law was given through Moses; grace and truth were realized through Jesus Christ" (John 1:17). Jesus' teaching confirmed the Holy Word of the Bible; there are no contradictions; only affirmations of a holy God. Jesus said, "For had ye believed Moses, ye would have believed me: for he wrote of me" (John 5:46). Lord, we thank you for the wisdom of the holy Book of Genesis; open our ears so that we may hear your instructions, open our minds so that we may grow in your wisdom, open our hearts so that we may help others, and strengthen our limbs so that we may walk in your path, Amen. We study Genesis inductively from the particular stories, and therefore we gain insight into the book as a whole. The first book of the Bible is a universal story about God and His truth, and it is constructed from its vividly told particular stories. His power, holiness, and sovereignty are a foundation for the rest of the Bible.

CHAPTER ELEVEN

Exodus and Moses: Man of God

In Exodus, we observe that God is revealing Himself to us through His Holy attributes. Exodus is the second book of the Holy Bible, and the title is derived from the Greek *Exodos*, meaning 'the going out' or 'exit' of the Israelites from Egypt. Exodus refers to the knowledge of God through personal experience, and centers on the relationship between God and Moses — with Moses as the message carrier, for God to the Israelites. We can apply Exodus to our own actions, i.e., our duty is to have faith in God's Word, to obey God's commandments, and to trust in the Holy Word (and there is no better teacher for this trust than Moses!). In reading Exodus, we become familiar with Moses at the burning bush (Ex 3:14-17), and grow to love the Lord as we follow the events that lead to the glory of the Lord filling the Holy Tabernacle (Ex 40:34-38). Moses acts as a mediator between God and the Israelites, and is responsible for making the Lord known to the Israelites. He is central in the role that establishes a covenant relationship that enables the Lord to dwell in the midst of the Israelites. God always makes the initiative and reveals Himself through words, wonders, and signs. He both speaks and acts, and what He says always happens. In practicing our inductive methodology that we have learned from Socrates, we 'interpret' Exodus as a revelation to us of the Holiness of God.

When we apply our inductive question of 'when' to Exodus, we discover that the historical setting and dates are difficult to determine. Some scholars place the Exodus as dealing with historical events in the second millennium B.C., while other scholars place the Israelites departure from Egypt in approximately 1446 B.C. Certain sections of Exodus were recorded by Moses (Ex 17:14; 24:4; 34:27), but there is little evidence to tell us whether the book was written many years after the events described, with the exception of the reference to the Israelites eating manna for forty years until they arrived in the land of Canaan (Ex 16:35). The traditional view by scholars is that Moses wrote the entire book. The book is a skillful narrative of different types of material: prose, poetry, genealogy, speeches, regulations, and laws. An analysis of the book reveals that it is composed of blocks of material that have a beginning and an end. We observe that a knowledge of the earlier material leads to an understanding of later events. The book is about knowing Yahweh through personal experience, and Moses acts as the mediator who first makes the Lord known to them. He acts as the liberator of the people of Israel, lawgiver, and leader of a group transformed by him from an unorganized and scattered community into a nation blessed and chosen by Yahweh.

He plays an important role in establishing the covenant relationship between God and the Israelites — this covenant relationship enables the Lord to dwell in the midst of His Chosen. God delights in a spiritual Israel who worships, loves, obeys, and is dutiful to the Lord. Moses declared the goodness of God to the children of Israel, and each challenge that they faced gave God the opportunity to demonstrate that He was providential, caring, protective, wise, faithful, true, steadfast, powerful, holy, and a loving Lord. The children of Israel experienced the power and love of the Lord on a continuous basis: with the manna that God provided them for forty years for their sustenance, with the quail (for food) that supernaturally came to them in the wilderness, with His Holy guidance (both physical and spiritual), with His Holy presence in the Temple of Moses, and with the rock from where water flowed to quench their thirst.

Exodus begins with a recital of the names of the twelve patriarchs. The number of Jacob's family was seventy souls when they went down into Egypt (Ex 1:5); and after the death of Joseph and all of his generation, the children of Israel were fruitful and they multiplied (Ex 1:6-7). The remarkable growth of the Israelites leads to the Egyptians fearing them, and they adopt inhumane measures to repress the Israelites. We learn the 'where' and 'what' of Exodus when we study and read that Egypt becomes a land of bondage for the children of Israel. We learn what is happening in the opening chapter of Exodus when the Bible tells us that the Israelites were oppressed by the Egyptians, but the more that they were oppressed the more they multiplied (Ex 1:12). We learn what action is taking place when we read that the midwives were ordered by Pharaoh to murder the male children of the Israelites (Ex 1:15-16). We learn the effect of the action when we read, "But the midwives feared God and did not as the King of Egypt commanded them" (Ex 1:17). The consequences of the midwives refusal to act were that God blessed the midwives for obedience to the Lord, and the people multiplied (Ex 1:20). Our inductive application of the story and the conclusion is that whenever man's laws contravene God's laws we must always obey Him.

Pharaoh gave orders to the Egyptians to drown all of the male children of the Israelites so that they would be destroyed (Ex 1:22). Through the cunning of Moses' mother, his life is saved after she places him on the river in a basket made of bulrushes (Ex 2:3). Pharaoh's daughter finds the baby, and names him Moses because he was drawn out of the water (Ex 2:3-10). He was adopted by Pharaoh's daughter, and grows up and is educated in an Egyptian court (Ex 2:9-10). The Bible tells us, "Moses was educated in all of the learning and wisdom of the Egyptians, and he was a man of power in words and deeds" (Acts 7:22). We read in Exodus that when Moses had grown up, he visited his brethren, the sons of Israel, and looked on their hard labors (Ex 2:11). The Exodus story is confirmed in Acts where it is written that Moses was forty years old when he visited his brethren (Acts 7:23). Moses kills an Egyptian who is beating an Israelite, and he is forced to flee and live in exile in the land of Midian (Ex 2:11-15). Moses meets the daughters of the priest of Midian at the well where he watered their flock (Ex 2:16-23) "So God heard their groaning; and God remembered His covenant with Abraham, Isaac, and Jacob" (Ex 2:24). Our application of this story is to remember that God is always there; "Ask, and it will be given to you..." (Mat 7:7). We inductively observe that the Old and New Testaments are harmonious and confirm God's Holy Word. The Old Testament Covenant is replaced by the New Testament, with the birth of Christ who holds the treasures of God's wisdom and knowledge (Col 2:3).

In Exodus, we observe that God reveals Himself to us through His Holy attributes and His miraculous actions. In chapter 3, He reveals what miraculous actions He intends to take on behalf of the oppressed Israelites. God commissioned Moses as the one to lead the Israelites out of Egyptian bondage. God communicates with Moses and the details of these holy encounters are written in the Bible for our edification. The first forty years of his life were spent as a prince in Pharaoh's court, and the second forty years in obscurity, tending Jethro's sheep. One day Moses led his flock to Mount Horeb (he was eighty years old), where God revealed (speaking through a burning thorny bush that was not consumed by the fire) his mission to him by calling his name, "Moses, Moses"; and Moses responded, "Here I am" (Ex 3:4). God reveals His Holiness to Moses by saying, "Remove your sandals from your feet, for the place on which you are standing is holy ground" (Ex 3:5). He acknowledges God's holiness by removing his sandals; however, he wants to know how he would convince the Israelites that God had sent him to them (Ex 3:13-15). Moses' request for God's name is important in our inductive study for the cultural context — the Israelites believed that the name reflected the person's essence. "I am the God of Abraham, the God of Isaac, and the God of Jacob" (Ex 3:5-6). The mention of the patriarchs would tell Moses that God had not forgotten the ancient promises that He had made in the Abrahamic Covenant. As we study the Bible inductively, we also learn to know His nature by the names used to designate Him: *El Elyon* (God Most High; Gn 14:18-20), *El Roi* (God who sees me; Gn 16:13), and *El Shaddai* (God Almighty; Gn 21:33). Here God introduced Himself by the personal name *Yahweh* translated as the Lord. The Hebrew divine name *Yahweh* is closely related to the phrase in verse 14 that is translated, *I AM WHO I AM*. *Yahweh* does not limit God's nature to any particular characteristic; He is what He is, His nature does not change. 'I am the one who always Is' or 'I will be who I will be' are a variety of translations, and they all teach us inductively about God's self-existence.

Throughout the Exodus story, the divine presence is frequently symbolized by fire and smoke (Ex 13:21-22; 19:18; 24:17). The flaming bush was a symbolic manifestation of an eternal God — as the bush that did not "burn up" it simply burned on — God is eternal, He does not end. He is holy; and His sanctity is a repeated theme in Exodus. The Creator's holiness sets Him apart from all created beings, and refers to His majesty and His perfect moral purity. God's holiness is the definition of what is pure and righteous in the entire universe. The Bible is the story of the revelation of Jesus Christ who brings man, a sinner, back to God, forgives him his sin, and makes him as holy as Jesus Christ. From an understanding of God's characteristics of His Holy and eternal nature, we utilize our inductive reasoning to conclude that God is an awesome and powerful entity; therefore, He must be approached with caution, and with a worshipful and loving attitude.

Moses hid his face, for he was afraid to look at God (Ex 3:6). Then the Lord said, "I have surely seen the affliction of My people who are in Egypt, and have given heed to their cry because of their taskmasters, for I am aware of their sufferings" (Ex 3:7). God tells Moses that He is sending him to deliver the Israelites out of Egypt, and to bring them to a land "flowing with milk and honey" (Ex 3:8; 17). The Israelites do not go directly to the promised land into Canaan but take a one-hundred and fifty mile detour to Mount Sinai (Ex 3:12). Moses asks God what he should tell the people, and who has sent him to deliver them, and He responds, "I AM WHO I AM" *(ego eimi)* (Ex 3:14). (The personal name of the Lord is YHWH, often pronounced as *Yahweh, Yahveh, or* Jehovah. God is instructing us that He is great and eternal.) He instructs Moses to petition Pharaoh for three days' vacation from their tasks so that they may worship the Lord outside of Egypt (Ex 3:18). God tells Moses that the king of Egypt will not let the Israelites go, therefore, He will strike Egypt with all of His miracles, and after that he will let you go (Ex 3: 19-20). We observe from our study of Exodus, that God is eternally present with us. He assures Moses of His continual presence with him as he went to Egypt to carry out the task that God has given him.

Moses was the person that God chose to deliver His people out of Egypt, but first he had to be instructed and disciplined in true fellowship and oneness with God. We may also have a vision of what He wants us to accomplish, but perhaps we have not yet been trained and disciplined for the mission. Just like Moses, we may have the love and desire to do our appointed work for God's Kingdom, but we may have doubts about our own abilities. In chapter 4, Moses doubts himself saying, "what if the people do not believe me?" (Ex 4:1). The Lord commands Moses to throw his staff on the ground, and then the Lord turned it into a serpent. Then the Lord directed Moses to grasp the serpent by the tail, and it turns back into a staff (Ex 4:3-4). Then He commands Moses to put his hand to his bosom, and it turns leprous like snow. When the Lord orders him to do so again, his hand is restored to flesh (Ex 4:6-7). The Lord tells Moses that if they do not believe after they witness these miracles, then Moses will be given a third one to perform (Ex 4:9). Moses still doubts his abilities, and claims that he has never been eloquent and he feels that he is slow of speech (Ex 4:10). The Lord responds that He will be with Moses' mouth and will teach him what to say (Ex 4:12). The Lord became angry with Moses for doubting; but He sends him to deliver His message to Pharaoh, and appoints Aaron, Moses' older brother (and prophet), to assist him (Ex 4:14). The Lord orders him to perform all of the miracles for Pharaoh and tells him that the He will harden Pharaoh's heart so that he will not let the Israelites go (Ex 4:21). God works through Moses to show His power, and he deals with his doubt by reassuring him that he will instruct him what to say. When we apply the Moses story to our own understanding, we learn that God's inspiration and guidance will manifest itself to us whenever we need help in any difficult situation.

In chapter 5, Moses and Aaron go to meet Pharaoh, demanding the unreceptive king to let the Israelites go to the wilderness so they may worship God and celebrate a feast in honor of the Lord (Ex 5:1). Pharaoh shows contempt toward Moses, Aaron, and God, proclaiming, "Who is the Lord that I should obey His voice to let Israel go?" (Ex 5:2). Then Pharaoh increases the work tasks of the Israelites to take their mind away from God and orders the foreman of the sons of Israel to be beaten, when they cannot complete this impossible task. The suffering Israelites go to Moses and complain that his words from the Lord have made them odious in Pharaoh's sight, and have, therefore, caused them much harm (Ex 5:21). Moses returns to the Lord and asks, "O Lord, why have You brought harm to this people, and you have not delivered your people at all" (Ex 5:22-23).

The Lord tells Moses that He will compel the ruler to drive the Israelites out of his land (Ex 6:1). God renewed His covenant promise that he made to Abraham, Isaac, and Jacob and explained, "I am the Lord; Almighty, but by My name, Lord, I did not make myself known to them" (Ex 6:3-4). He also tells Moses that He will bring the Israelites to the covenant land as He has sworn before to Abraham, Isaac, and Jacob (Ex 6:8).

Therefore, Moses speaks to the Israelites again but they do not listen because of their despondency and cruel bondage (Ex 6:9). The Lord again instructs Moses to go to Pharaoh and ask him to let the Israelites go (Ex 6:11). The Bible then enumerates a genealogy of the heads of their fathers' households — of the sons of Israel (Ex 6:14-25). The Lord commanded Moses to speak to Pharaoh and Moses responds (still doubting his abilities) how will Pharaoh listen to him he is unskilled in speech? (Ex 6:29-30).

God reassures Moses, "See, I make you as God to Pharaoh, and your brother Aaron shall be your prophet" (Ex 7:1). Aaron was Moses' prophet, and acted as a message carrier from one of greater authority i.e., Moses, who was God's prophet. When we put this into context, we observe that the function of a prophet is established through Moses. The prophet approached men as God's ambassador, and showed men their sins and urged them to turn away from their evil ways. This has direct application to us for the new Covenant, as Apostle Paul writes, "Therefore, we are ambassadors for Christ, as though God were making an appeal through us; we beg you on behalf of Christ, be reconciled to God. He made Him who knew no sin to be sin on our behalf, so that we might become the righteousness of God in Him" (2 Cor 5:20-21).

Then God directs Moses to go to Pharaoh and tell him to let the sons of Israel go out of Egypt, and He gives Moses great power and authority to complete his mission (Ex 7:2). God tells Moses that He will harden Pharaoh's heart so that He may multiply His signs and wonders in the land of Egypt so that the Egyptians may know that He is Lord (Ex 7:3, 5). The Lord tells Moses that when Pharaoh asks him to perform a miracle that he is to throw down his staff and it will become a serpent (Ex 7:9). Moses and Aaron do what God commands, yet Pharaoh's heart was still hardened. Pharaoh called the wise men and the magicians to do the same thing with their rod using their secret arts, but Aaron's rod swallowed up their staffs (Ex 7:12). The Lord commanded Moses to go to the Nile and say unto Pharaoh, "By this you shall know that I am the LORD," and Moses strikes the water of the Nile with his staff and the water turns to blood (Ex 7:17). The blood was over the bodies of all the waters of Egypt, so that all the fish died and the water source became foul (Ex 7:21). Pharaoh's heart was still hardened (Ex 7:22). We observe from the Bible that the plague continued for seven difficult days (Ex 7:25).

The Lord tells Moses to go to Pharaoh and demand him "to let My people go, that they may serve me" (Ex 8:1), and He instructs Moses to tell Pharaoh that if he refuses, then he will strike the whole land of Egypt with frogs (Ex 8:2). Aaron stretched out his hand with his rod and the frogs came up and covered the land of Egypt (Ex 7:6). Pharaoh says that if Moses will remove the frogs, then he will let the people go, but when there was relief from the frogs, Pharaoh again hardened his heart (Ex 8:15). Then the Lord sent the plague of gnats into the lands of Egypt (Ex 8:17). Pharaoh still would not relent, so the Lord sent the plague of flies into the lands of Egypt (Ex 8:21). Pharaoh dealt deceitfully with Moses —

and again hardened his heart — and would not let the people go (Ex 8:32).

Then the Lord tells Moses that He will visit Egypt with a plague of pestilence on the livestock: the horses, the donkeys, camels, herds and flocks (Ex 9:3). The livestock of the sons of Israel, however, were not touched by the pestilence. The Lord then sent the plague of boils on man and beast throughout Egypt (Ex 9:9). Moses then stretched out his hand toward the sky and God rained down hail and fire on all the land of Egypt (Ex 9:22). A contrite Pharaoh divulges to Moses that he has sinned and the Lord is the righteous one, so he will let your people go (Ex 9:27-28). However, when Pharaoh saw that the hail, fire, and thunder had ceased, he hardened his heart again (Ex 9:34-35).

After Moses announced that the Lord was going to send a plague of locusts, Pharaoh's officials tried to persuade him to reconsider his position. With Pharaoh's heart hardened, the Lord visited the lands of Egypt with the plague of locusts. The locusts covered the whole land, so that the land was darkened; and they ate every plant and fruit of the trees (Ex 10:15). Pharaoh relents and calls for Moses to remove the plagues and promises to release the Israelites. However, after the shifting wind from the Lord removed the locusts, Pharaoh again hardened his heart (Ex 10:20), so Moses stretches out his hand following the Lord's instructions, causing a thick darkness to cover the land of Egypt for three days (Ex 10:23). The sons of Israel, however, had light in their dwellings (Ex 10:23). Pharaoh threatens to kill Moses, and again hardened his heart and would not let the Lord's people go (Ex 10:10).

While still in Pharaoh's presence, Moses receives a revelation from God that every firstborn son in Egypt will die (Ex 11:5). Moses performed all of these miracles before Pharaoh yet the Lord hardened Pharaoh's heart, and he did not let the Israelites go. In Exodus 12, God instructs the Israelites on how to observe the Passover. "For I will go through the land of Egypt on that night, and will strike down all the firstborn in the land of Egypt, both man and beast;...The blood shall be a sign for you on the houses where you live; and when I see the blood I will pass over you..." (Ex 12:12-13). At midnight, the Lord struck all the firstborn in Egypt, from the firstborn of Pharaoh...to the firstborn of the captive...and the firstborn of cattle (Ex 12:29). There was a great cry in Egypt, and Pharaoh called Moses and told him to go and worship the Lord (Ex 12:30-31). The Israelites took unleavened bread, articles of silver and gold, and clothing from the Egyptians (as the Lord had requested), and they journeyed to Succoth (Ex 12:34-37). The Lord gives Moses the ordinance for respecting the Passover that was to be celebrated as a permanent reminder of the necessity of blood to avert God's wrath (Ex 12:43-51). The Lord gives divine instructions to the Israelites for selecting a Passover lamb. The Passover was the redemptive moment in history when the Lord executed judgment against all of the gods of Egypt (Ex 12:12). In conjunction with the Passover was the Feast of the Unleavened Bread, which is celebrated immediately following Passover for seven days, commencing on *Aviv* (or *Nisan*) 15. The Lord instructed the Israelites, "Seven days you shall eat unleavened bread, but on the first day you shall remove leaven from your houses; for whoever eats anything leavened from the first day until the seventh day, that person shall be cut off from Israel" (Ex 12:15). The Lord instructs the Israelites that they shall observe this rite forever (Ex 12:24).

We observe (using induction) that the Passover has symbolic significance for our understanding of the Lord. In the New Testament, Apostle John writes, "Behold the Lamb of God who takes away the sin of the world" (John 1:29). The imagery of the unblemished sacrificial Passover lamb refers to Jesus, "Worthy is the Lamb that was slain to receive power and riches and wisdom and might and honor and glory and blessing" (Rv 5:12). "Knowing that you were not redeemed with perishable things like silver or gold from your futile way of life inherited from your forefathers, but with precious blood, as of a lamb unblemished and spotless, the blood of Christ" (1 Pt 1: 18-19). We observe the Lord's instructions that no bones should be broken on the Passover lamb. Apostle John writes, "For these things shall come to pass to fulfill the Scripture, 'Not a bone of Him shall be broken' " (John 19:36).

We interpret (using induction) Exodus as teaching us that God had several purposes in mind when He visited Egypt with the ten plagues. The first was to compel Pharaoh to release the Hebrews from bondage. In Genesis 12, verse 3, God states that He will curse those who curse Israel; hence, Egypt is punished for the harsh treatment of the Hebrews. "For this time I will send all

My plagues on you and your servants and your people, so that you may know that there is no one like Me in all the earth," said the Lord (Ex 9:16). God showed His absolute authority and power to the Israelites — and to the Egyptians — when He visited Egypt with the ten plagues. There were over eighty ancient Egyptian gods representing some animal or object, and Pharaoh was considered the incarnation of the god Horus. The plagues challenged the Egyptian pantheon of gods and demonstrated that the Lord was superior over false gods.

God teaches us through holy symbols so that we may learn of His Holy love for us. The Lord spoke to Moses and told him that the firstborn is sanctified to God (Ex 13:1-2). The pillar of cloud — God's presence and symbolic of His protection and power — moved before them and stood between them and the Egyptians (Ex 13:21). God directed the Israelites to camp before Pihahiroth, and the Egyptians pursued them (Ex 14:2-8). When Moses stretched out his hand over the Red Sea, the Lord sent an east wind that parted the waters so that the Israelites could pass through the sea on dry land (Ex 14:27). When the people saw the great power of the Lord, they feared Him and believed in the Lord and His servant Moses (Ex 14:31).

Moses and the sons of Israel sang a song to the Lord for the deliverance. "I will sing to the LORD, for He is highly exalted; The horse and its rider He has hurled into the sea" (Ex 15:1). "Who is like You among the gods, O LORD? Who is like You, majestic in holiness, Awesome in praises, working wonders?" (Ex 15:11). "In Your loving kindness You have led the people whom You have redeemed; In Your strength You have guided them to Your holy habitation" (Ex 15:13). "Miriam the prophetess, Aaron's sister, took the timbrel in her hand, and all the women went out after her with timbrels and with dancing. Sing to the Lord, for He is highly exalted..." (Ex 15:20-21). When the Israelites came to Marah, they could not drink the water because it was bitter, so the Lord sweetened the waters for them (Ex 15:23-25). Then the Israelites came to Elim where there were springs of water and date palms, and they camped there (Ex 15:27).

Then the Israelites sojourned to the wilderness of Sin where they grumbled against Moses and Aaron for there was no food (Ex 16:1-3). The Lord promises to send manna and quails from heaven (Ex 16:12-14). The Lord gave them particular instructions respecting the manna, and an omer of manna was to be preserved (Ex 16:16-34). The Israelites ate the manna for forty years until they came to the border of the land of Canaan (Ex 16:35). The Bible tells us that at Rephidim the Israelites murmur for water, and the Lord instructs Moses to strike a rock with his staff and water came out of the rock so that the people may drink (Ex 17:5-6). The Israelites fought against the Amaleks and won with the Lord's help; and Moses built an altar to the Lord and prayed, "The Lord is my Banner" (Ex 17:13-16).

Moses' father-in-law, Jethro — who was the priest of Midian — came to Moses with Moses' wife and children (Ex 18:1-2). Moses entertains Jethro, and Jethro gives counsel to Moses by telling him that he will wear himself out by acting as the sole judge and representative of all the Israelites. Jethro advises Moses that he should appoint men out of all Israel and make them heads over the people for minor disputes, and that they were to bring the difficult disputes to Moses who would then bring these to God (Ex 18:18-27).

In the third month, the Israelites came into the wilderness of Sinai. The Lord God transforms Mount Sinai in a symbolic show of His power and glory, and explains to Moses that He would come to them in a thick cloud, so that the people could hear him speak and believe in Him forever (Ex 19:9). The Lord instructs Moses to tell the people to consecrate themselves for on the third day the He will come down on Mount Sinai in the sight of them (Ex 19:9-11). It was all in smoke and on fire as the Lord descended upon it, and the mountain quaked violently as the Lord called Moses to the top (Ex 19: 18-20). Then God revealed the words of the Ten Commandments to him declaring (Ex 20), "All the people perceived the thunder and the lighting flashes and the sound of the trumpet and the mountain smoking; and when the people saw it, they trembled and stood at a distance" (Ex 19:18). The people hear the voice of God, "I am the Lord your God, who brought you out of Egypt, and out of the land of slavery." Then what followed is a list of stipulations that were to form the basis of Israel's covenant relationship with God (Ex 20:3-17). Why the Israelites were to obey these commands is answered — out of their love and obedience for God! Moses and the elders of Israel "saw the God of Israel; and under His feet there appeared to be a pavement of sapphire, as clear as the night itself" (Ex 24:10). Exodus 21 and 22 gives the judicial laws and we can inductively interpret that this shows God's concern for justice for His people. Moses recorded everything that God said in the Book of the Covenant (Ex 24:7). God gives the Israelites laws against falsehood and injustice, the year of rest, the Sabbath, and the three festivals (Ex 24). God promised to conduct the Israelites to Canaan if they remained obedient to the Lord (Ex 23:22-23).

Then the Lord said to Moses, "Come up to the Lord, you and Aaron, Nadab and Abihu, and seventy of the elders of Israel, and you shall worship at a distance" (Ex 24:1). "Now the Lord said to Moses, 'Come up to me on the mountain and remain there and I will give you the stone tablets with the law and the commandments which I have written for their instruction' " (Ex 24:12). Therefore, Moses went up to the mountain of God with Joshua his servant (Ex 24:13). Moses spends forty days and nights on the mountain (Ex 24:18). The Lord instructed Moses to raise a contribution for incense for Him with gold, silver and bronze, fine linens, skins, oil for lighting, spices for the anointing oil, onyx and setting stones for the breastplate for the high priest (Ex 25:1-7). We observe (using induction) from the Bible that these were all of the precious materials that God had instructed the Israelites to carry out of Egypt with them on the Exodus. The Lord instructs the Israelites to construct a tabernacle for Him so that He may dwell among them (Ex 25:8). God gives them the pattern of the tabernacle and all of its furniture, and the instructions on how they were to construct the Ark of the Covenant (Ex 25:10). The Lord instructs Moses to make everything for the tabernacle after the pattern that was shown to Moses on the mountain (Ex 25:40). Every article in the tabernacle was to be made specifically to God's instructions, including the dimensions, the material, and the functions. The instructions for the holy garment, the *ephod*, to be worn by the high priest is given in chapter 28; and we can visualize the holy garment with the precious inlaid stones created by skilled craftsman, and the holy selection — the time when God appoints the sons of Israel who are to minister as priests for Him. Aaron and his sons are set apart for the priest's office. We inductively observe that the priest's function was to approach God on behalf of the people, and to bring man and God into a relationship with one another. The Bible gives us a description of the priestly garments: the ephod, the breastplate, the Urim and Thummim, the robe of the *ephod*, the plate of the mitre, and the garments for Aaron's sons (Ex 28). God promises to dwell among Israel, and He instructs them to sacrifice a bull and two rams without blemish for burnt offerings to consecrate the priests (Ex 29). The Lord tells Moses, "They shall know that I am the Lord their God who brought them out of the land of Egypt, that I might dwell among them; I am the Lord their God" (Ex 29:46). We can interpret (through induction) the meaning: God desires to dwell in the midst of His redeemed people in His own sanctuary and on His own terms. We can apply this to our Christian lives by remembering that God is holy, and His desire to dwell with us leads us to strive for holiness with singleness of heart and purity of service to the Lord.

On Mount Sinai, Moses is given the tablets of the law written by the finger of God (Ex 31:18). When Moses was delayed coming down from the Mount, the people — led by Aaron — made an idolatrous golden calf to worship. The Israelites had witnessed God's triumph over Egypt at the exodus, and the parting of the Red Sea, and they had witnessed the spectacular manifestations of God's presence on the mountain. Aaron and his sons, and seventy of the elders, were privileged to eat a meal in God's presence! Yet, with the short absence of Moses, they made an idol to worship in disobedience to what God had commanded them not to do. God was displeased, and He sent Moses down from the Mount so he could intercede. In anger, Moses breaks the tablets of the law and destroys the golden calf, and then he prays for the people (Ex 32). He prays and reminds the Lord that despite His wrath, these are still Your people whom he has brought out of bondage from Egypt (Ex 32:11). Moses further implores that the Egyptians will think that the Lord had evil intent to bring the Hebrews out of Egypt, only to kill the people in the mountains (Ex 32:12). Moses reminds the Lord about the Abrahamic Covenant and His oath to the patriarchs about both seed and land (Ex 32:13), and He urges, "If now I have found favor in Your sight, O Lord, I pray, let the Lord go along in our midst, even though the people are so obstinate, and pardon our sin..." (Ex 34:9). The Lord responded that He would make a covenant with the people and perform miracles for them (Ex 34:10). The Lord promises to drive out the Amorite, the Canaanite, the Hittite, the Perizzite, the Hivite, and the Jebusite (Ex 34:11). The tablets of the law are renewed after Moses' entreaty, and God's covenant is renewed; He then directs Moses in the observance of the Feast of Unleavened Bread, the Feast of Weeks, the Feast of Ingathering, and the Feast of the Passover (Ex 34:18-25). Moses was with the Lord for forty days and forty nights, and during this time, he did not eat bread or drink water. When Moses came down from Mount Sinai with the Ten Commandments in his hand, the skin of his face shone because he had been speaking with God (Ex 34:28-29).

Moses spoke to the entire congregation and instructed them on the things that the Lord commanded them to do (Ex 35:1). The Sabbath was to be observed; the freewill offerings for the sanctuary materials were to be contributed; and the readiness of the people skilled by the Lord, and Bezaleel, Aholliab, and every skilled person "in whom the Lord has put skill and understanding to know how to perform all the work in the construction of the sanctuary" (Ex 36:1). The Israelites' hearts were stirred and their spirits were moved by the Lord to construct the sanctuary (Ex 35). God was the divine architect of the sanctuary, and Moses, Bezaleel, and Aholliab built it according to the Divine Pattern. And the Lord called the sons and daughters of Israel, for example, Bezaleel: "And He has filled him with the Spirit of God, in wisdom, in understanding and in knowledge and in all craftsmanship; to make designs for working in gold and in silver and in bronze" (Ex 35:31-32). The Tabernacle took nine months to build, and when it was completed, it became the dwelling place of the Lord (Ex 19:1; Nm 9:1).

The Lord commands Moses to instruct the children of Israel to bring freewill offerings: gold, silver, brass, and fine linens of blue, purple, and scarlet, goat's hair, ram's skins dyed red, badger's skins, shittim wood, oil for light, spices for anointing oil, sweet incense, onyx stones, and stones to be set in the ephod and the breastplate (Ex 25:1-7; 35:4-9). The materials required by the Lord were those taken from the mineral, plant and animal kingdoms.[87] God has hidden Divine and eternal Truths in the order, materials, dimensions, and colors of the Tabernacle of Moses. We understand the heavenly Kingdom by the symbolism God reveals to us in the natural realm. In the mineral kingdom, gold is symbolic of the Glory of God and His Divine nature — gold is a precious metal and incorruptible. The items in the Most Holy place within the Tabernacle were covered with gold, for example, the Ark of the Covenant, the mercy seat, and the cherubim. The Lord speaks to Moses saying, "They shall construct an ark of acacia wood two and a half cubits long, and one and a half cubits wide, and one and a half cubits high. You shall overlay it with pure gold, inside and out you shall overlay it, and you shall make a gold molding around it" (Ex 25:10-11). God instructs Moses, "You shall make a mercy seat of pure gold, two and a half cubits long and one and a half cubits wide" (Ex 25:17). "You shall make two cherubim of gold, make them of hammered work at the two ends of the mercy seat" (Ex 25:18). The Lord continued saying, "You shall make a plate of pure gold and shall engrave on it, like the engravings of a seal, 'Holy to the Lord' " (Ex 28:36). "Then you shall make a lampstand of pure gold" (Ex 25:31). We observe and remember that the Bible teaches us that the streets of the Holy City of New Jerusalem are paved with pure gold (Rev 21:21).

Silver symbolizes redemption and atonement; we observe that Christ — who was our ransom — was betrayed for thirty pieces of silver (Ex 30:11-16; 1 Peter 1:18-20). Brass symbolizes God and the Holy Spirit, and His strength and judgment against sin. When the Israelites sinned against the Lord by questioning Him and complaining, "Why have you brought us up out of Egypt to die in the wilderness? For there is no food and no water; and we loathe this miserable food" (Num 21:5). The Lord sent fiery serpents among the people and many people of Israel died (Num 21:6). The people came to Moses and confessed that they had sinned against the Lord, and they asked Moses to intercede that He may remove the serpents from them. The Lord instructed Moses to make a fiery serpent and set it on a standard, and anyone who is bitten will look at it and live (Num 21:7-8). "And Moses made a bronze serpent and set it on the standard; and it came about, that if a serpent bit any man, when he looked to the bronze serpent, he lived" (Num 21:9). God tells us that if we do not listen to His voice, then the heavens will be as brass (Deut 28:13-23).

The holy garments for Aaron's sons (Nadab and Abihu, Eleazar and Ithamar) — to minister as priests to the Lord — were also made with precious materials following the Lord's instructions. "These are the garments that they shall make: a breastplate and an ephod and a robe and a tunic of checkered work, a turban and a sash..." (Ex 28:4). "You shall make a breastplate of judgment, the work of a skillful workman; like the work of the ephod you shall make it: of gold, of blue and purple and scarlet material and fine twisted linen you shall make it" (Ex 28:15). "You shall mount on it four rows of stones; the first row shall be a row of ruby, topaz and emerald; and the second row a turquoise, a sapphire and a diamond; and the third row a jacinth, an agate and an amethyst; and the fourth row a beryl and an onyx and a jasper; they shall be set in gold filigree. The stones shall be according to the names of the sons of Israel: twelve, according to their names; they shall be like the engravings of a seal, each according to his name for the twelve tribes" (Ex 28:15-21). The precious stones on the priestly garments symbolize the various gifts of the Holy Spirit, the glories of the saints, and God's love for the Israelites, and the righteousness of the children of God.

The materials of the Tabernacle relating to the plant kingdom are fine linen, shittim wood, oil for light, spices for anointing oil, and spices for sweet incense. Fine linen is symbolic of our Lord and His righteousness. Shittim wood was indestructible like the nature of our Lord: immortal and sinless. Oil is symbolic of the Holy Spirit and it is used in connection with light. The Holy Spirit enlightens our eyes and gives us intellectual understanding and heart wisdom of our Lord. The spices for anointing oil symbolize the different operations of the Holy Spirit who consecrates us to minister in His name. The spices for sweet incense symbolize the different types of prayer or homage: intercession, praise, and worship of the Lord. "When He had taken the book, the four living creatures and the twenty-four elders fell down before the Lamb, each one holding a harp and golden bowls full of incense, which are the prayers of the saints. And they sang a new song saying, 'Worthy are You to take the book and to break its seals; for You were slain, and purchased for God with Your blood men from every tribe and tongue and people and nation. You have made them to be a kingdom and priests to our God; and they will reign upon earth' " (Rev 5:8-10).

The materials of the Tabernacle relating to the animal kingdom are blue (shellfish), purple (shellfish), scarlet (worm or insect), goat's hair, ram's skin dyed red, and badger's skins. The color blue is associated with the Tabernacle and the furnishings. "Moreover you shall make the tabernacle with ten curtains of fine twisted linen and blue and purple and scarlet material; you shall make them with cherubim, the work of a skillful workman" (Ex 26:1). The Ark of the Covenant was covered with a blue cloth symbolic of its close association with the Word of God (Num 4:5-7, 11-13). The robe of the High Priest was blue symbolic of the close association with God and His Word (Ex 28:31-33). The sky blue color of sapphire represents heavenly things (Ez 1:26). Blue is associated with the Lord's commandments to us (Num 15:38-40). Scarlet is the color of blood and symbolizes the sacrifice that our Lord made for us. It is the color symbolic of the redemptive work of our Lord, and the Atonement when He became the sacrifice and shed His blood for our sins. Goat's hair is symbolic of the sin offering in the Old Testament. Ram's skin symbolizes consecration, dedication, and substitution; Abraham offered a ram as a sacrifice to the Lord instead of his son Isaac. Badger's skins were used on the outside of the

Tabernacle to protect it; an observer would not know what preciousness was hidden on the inside; just as an observer would not perceive the preciousness of our Lord unless they were aware that His beauty is hidden behind the external. "Who has believed our message? And to whom has the arm of the Lord been revealed? For He grew up before Him like a tender shoot, And like a root out of parched ground; He has no stately form or majesty That we should look upon Him, nor appearance that we should be attracted to Him, He was despised and forsaken of men, A man of sorrows and acquainted with grief; And like one from whom men hide their face He was despised, and we did not esteem Him" (Isa 53:1-3). "Oh, give ear, Shepherd of Israel, You who lead Joseph like a flock; You who are enthroned above the cherubim, shine forth!" (Psalms 80:1).

We inductively observe the Arks in the Bible, and we find God and His Holy hand of preservation at work in the relationship between our Father, man, and the Ark. The Biblical Arks are symbolic of preservation — from the first Ark that carried Noah, eight souls, and the animals and preserved them from the waters of the flood. The Tabernacle of Moses or the Ark of the Covenant symbolizes God's presence with the Israelites and His preservation of His chosen people. The Ark of the Covenant was also a place of preservation for the Tablets of the Law (Ex 25:21), the Golden Pot of Manna (Ex 16:33-34), and Aaron's rod that Budded (Num 17:10). "He (Moses) erected the court all around the tabernacle and the altar, and hung up the veil for the gateway of the court. Thus, Moses finished the work. Then the cloud covered the tent of meeting, and the glory of the Lord filled the tabernacle" (Ex 40:33-34). Moses made everything according to God's commands and the pattern that God revealed to Moses. From that moment on, the Glory-Cloud of the Lord led and governed the Israelites on their pilgrimage in the wilderness, speaking with them from above the mercy seat (Ex 25:22), and the Ark was the place for enquiring after the Lord concerning His will (Josh 20:18-28). Everything in the Old Testament finds fulfillment in the Lord Jesus Christ, who is our Ark, and the mediator for us with the Lord (1 Tim 2:5). "Moses said, The Lord God will raise up for you a prophet like me from your brethren; to Him you shall give heed to everything He says to you" (Acts 3:22). The final Ark mentioned in the Bible is the Ark of His Testament seen in heaven. "And the temple of God which is in heaven was opened; and the ark of his covenant appeared in His temple, and there were flashes of lightening and sounds and peals of thunder and an earthquake and a great hailstorm" (Rev 11:19). God will preserve those who are in Christ!

In the last chapters of Exodus, we read about the construction of the tabernacle and its furniture, the making of the ark, the brazen altar and laver, the court, and the offerings of the people (Ex 36-38). When Christ taught the disciples that the Law of Moses, the Psalms, and the Prophets must be fulfilled concerning Him, we can inductively conclude that the revelation of the Tabernacle is part of the law of Moses, and therefore contains prophecy concerning Christ (Luke 24:26). Christ taught, "For if you believed Moses, you would believe Me, for he wrote about Me" (John 5:46). God speaks to us through the Tabernacle of Moses, wherein the symbols of the natural elements of creation used in the Tabernacle represent the eternal truths of God. We comprehend abstract elements of truth if we have a material representation that we can understand. Therefore, the Tabernacle is full of types, i.e., shadows — and the shadow of a thing has no reality in and of itself, it just points us to the real substance. These material symbols represented by a type are our lessons to learn in order to understand the divine mystery of our Lord. When the Lord instructed Moses on the building of the Tabernacle He said, "There I will meet with you; and from above the mercy seat, from between the two cherubim which are upon the ark of the testimony, I will speak to you about all that I will give you in commandment for the sons of Israel" (Ex 25:22). When Moses finished the work of building the Tabernacle, the Bible tells us, "then the cloud covered the tent of meeting, and the glory of the Lord filled the tabernacle" (Ex 40:34). We observe from that moment on and for four centuries, the nation of Israel was led and governed by the Glory-Cloud of the Lord.

Moses stood at the head of the Hebrew nation as its leader for forty years. He acted as a priest during the temporary worship at Mount Sinai (Ex 24:1-8), and he acted as a priest at the consecration of Aaron and his sons (Lev 8:1-30). He was a poet and composed the song of triumph when they crossed the Red Sea (Ex 15:1-9), a song of gratitude in the wilderness (Neh 21:15-18), and his farewell song (Deut 32:1-44). We can inductively interpret Moses' character from his particular (and many) actions that he was a man who exhibited a noble and pure character throughout his lifetime, and was dutifully obedient to God. He refused to be called the son of Pharaoh's daughter. He was a learned man educated "in all the learning of the Egyptians, and he was a man of power in words and deeds" (Acts 7:22). He received his commission to deliver the Israelites from bondage directly from God. He had patience, "he supposed that his brethren understood that God was granting them deliverance through him, but they did not understand" (Acts 7:25). He loved his brethren and suffered affliction with the people of God (Ex 2:11-12; Heb 11:23-27). He was humble minded and tried to be excused from the leadership of his people (Ex 3:7-22; Ex 4:1-13). As a young leader, he was worshipful, loving and thankful to the Lord. "Who is like You among the gods, O Lord? Who is like You, majestic in holiness, Awesome in praises, working wonders?" (Gn 15:11). He patiently sat and heard all of the complaints of the Israelites from morning until night and passed judgment upon them, which demonstrates that he possessed great perseverance. He listened to the advice of others, for example, when his father-in-law, Jethro, advised him in reference to the government of the people; he took his advice (Ex 32:19-28). He was aggressive when he came down from the mountain with God's Holy writing engraved on the stone tablets and found the Israelites were worshipping a golden calf, "Moses' anger burned, and he threw the tablets from his hands and shattered them at the foot of the mountain" (Ex 32:19). He was compassionate and unselfish, when he petitioned the Lord to spare Israel when they sinned against Yahweh by worshipping the golden calf (Ex 32:9-13). Moses exhibited a noble and pure character throughout his lifetime.

We learn from his story that God guides us by His servants. We observed that He guided Moses and disciplined his heart, mind, and spirit to act as a servant of God. We can apply the lessons of Moses when we reflect on the fact that he had a period of loneliness in life when he was in apprenticeship, and then mastership for the work of the Lord. We can apply the lessons of Exodus to our own lives when we observe that God kept his distance from the stiff-necked Israelites due to their sin, but drew closer to Moses. Moses had an intimacy with God that was not seen since Adam and the Garden of Eden. What set him apart from the other Israelites was his extraordinary faith in God — a faith that continues to inspire us as we apprentice on our journey to discern His will.

CHAPTER TWELVE

Socrates, Love and the Symposium

The similarities between Socrates and Christ are bound together with love; love toward our fellow men and women, and love toward our Creator. God is love; and his affection fulfills all His laws. Socrates was born in a pre-Christian era but his message was one of love — the universal language. Our western culture often associates the word with physical love, but many also seek its essence. Socrates had his own unique view, associating it with moral actions of human beings, and the gods' acceptance of these actions. For him, love is also associated with beauty: the beauty of souls, the beauty of laws, activities, and customs, and the beauty of knowledge, ideas, and theories, and the Form of Beauty itself. To understand his view, it is helpful if we participate in an ancient Greek symposium along with Socrates, himself, so step back in time with me for an evening of entertainment.

The ancient Greek symposium was a male aristocratic social activity, taking place in the evening where the men drank together in a convivial atmosphere while they ate, conversed, recited poetry, played music, joked, gossiped, or performed games of skill and balance, while being entertained by professional dancers and courtesans. The status and wealth of the host was indicated by his guest list, as well as the quality of the food and the serving vessels. The symposium consisted of two parts: the first was dedicated to the food, generally simple fare, followed by the second, which was dedicated to drinking. The wine was accompanied by snacks that included chestnuts, beans, toasted wheat and honey cakes. By the late sixth century B.C., symposium vessels included wine coolers, jugs, drinking cups, and mixing vessels decorated with scenes, for example, Dionysus and his followers. The symposiarch (the master of ceremonies) would mix the wine to water in a strength that he determined, usually three or four parts water to one part wine. The wine was mixed in a large krater, and then slave boys filled pitchers from the krater and poured the drink into each participant's cup.

The *Symposium* is a dialogue written by Plato (no later than 385 B.C.) that discusses the events of a 'symposium' or a formal drinking party held in honor of Agathon in 416 B.C., a tragedian who had just successfully produced his first victorious tragedy. The gatherers reflect that the god of Love is neglected, so they honor the god with speeches and praise of "Love" (*eros*). The focus of the *Symposium* (written in a narrative structure) is the adult male's role as ethical and intellectual educator of the adolescent male.

The symposium was a gathering of Athenian men at a private home where they could relax reclined on cushions — usually one to two men on a couch — and discuss values while enjoying a social event that also liberated them from the everyday restraints of a regulated environment. The symposium we are invited to took place at Agathon's house. Among his guests were Socrates, Phaedrus, Pausanias, Eryximachus, Aristophanes, and Aristodemus. Aristodemus, a great admirer of Socrates, relays the events to Apollodorus, who in turn tells the story to the unnamed Athenian in Plato's *Symposium*. Aristodemus explains that he ran into Socrates, "who had just bathed and was looking so good. Socrates replied, 'I am going to Agathon's for dinner. I managed to avoid yesterday's victory party—I really don't like crowds—but I promised to be there today. So, naturally, I took great pains with my appearance: I'm going to the house of a good-looking man; I had to look my best.' "[88] On the way to the symposium, Socrates was delayed for he had stopped on a porch to meditate until the banquet was half over. (He frequently drifted off in philosophical reverie, remaining motionless while receiving philosophical wisdom.)

The plan for the evening was to discuss the nature of love, a subject not addressed as frequently as it should be, noted Eryximachus. The young man Phaedrus began the recitations stating that Love was the most ancient, most honored of gods and therefore the most capable of ensuring courage and happiness in this life and the next. He emphasized the importance of its guidance to us living a better life and declared that it was even more important and influential than many things, including family, state, or money. Furthermore, he proclaimed that Love teaches us shame when acting disgracefully and pride when we act well. He went along to suggest that an army that consisted solely of lovers and loved ones would be unmatchable, as they would rather die than show cowardice in front of a partner, striving constantly for greater honor. Phaedrus noted that Love may breathe into us the spirit of being a hero, "Love alone makes men ready to die for another's sake; and not men only, but women."[89] Phaedrus provided several examples of brave and honorable actions, as he recalled the story of Alcestis, who was willing to die for her husband Admetus. Apollo tells Admetus that he was to die unless he could find someone to die in his place. Not even his parents would accept the responsibility; however, Alcestis did, impressing the gods so much that they brought her back to life. By contrast, Phaedrus explained, Orpheus did not have the courage to die for his love, Eurydice, but descended into Hades to find her while still alive. As a result, he returned empty-handed and was later killed by the Maenads. In another example, he reiterated the story of Achilles, the great hero of the Iliad, who was the loved one of Patroclus, who was slain by Hector. It was prophesied that Achilles would be killed himself if he murdered Hector, but nonetheless Achilles still hunted down and killed the man who had slain his lover. Thus, Achilles showed supreme courage in accepting death in order to avenge his lover so the gods sent him to the islands of the blessed when he died. Phaedrus states, "In truth, the gods honor virtue most highly when it belongs to Love.", and concludes, "Love is the oldest god, and to be honored, and love helps men most to be in possession of virtue and happiness" (Sy*mposium* 180b).

Pausanias begins his turn with a discourse about heavenly love (the elder Aphrodite, daughter of Uranus) as opposed to the vulgar/common love (the younger Aphrodite, daughter of Zeus and Dione) and informs Phaedrus that while his speech was agreeable, the subject of love had not been well defined. Love, he continued, does not always bring out the best in us and while we may speak of it, we may not be implying the same thing. He argues that loving is in itself neither good nor bad. Worthy Love is of the mind, freeing us from all wantonness, while the vulgar Love is sensual and of the flesh and is worthless, inconsistent, and fleeting. The love of the virtuous character abides throughout life, so its main purpose is to produce virtue, and love pursued for any other means is wrong, regardless of the consequence.

Aristophanes was to speak next, however he developed the hiccups, so Eryximachus, a medical doctor, commenced, thanking Pausanias for distinguishing between two different kinds of love, but suggests that he limited himself when he considered all love to be emotional responses between human beings. Eryximachus' medical training demonstrated that love is expressed in the bodily responses of plants and animals. He agrees with Pausanias that it is right to gratify good people and wrong to gratify bad ones, and further explains that one should try to gratify the healthy parts of the body while depriving the diseased parts of any satisfaction so that they will cease to be diseased. The doctor's role, then, is to implant the healthy kind of love while flushing the harmful in order to reconcile and create love between the antagonistic elements of the body. He also adds that athletics, agriculture, and music are all wholly governed by the god of Love and insisted that both harmony and rhythm in music consist in creating agreement between divergent notes and tempos. Medicine too creates a similar agreement between divergent elements of the body, and therefore all creation of agreement and concord is a product of Love. Eryximachus concludes that Love is ever-present and all-powerful in our lives, and is the cause of all self-control, happiness, and justice, producing good actions. Eryximachus suggests that if he has left anything out of his eulogy, then Aristophanes can fill in the gaps, now that his hiccups have subsisted, due to Eryximachus' sneezing cure. In return, Aristophanes playfully remarks that it is odd that the well-ordered part of his body must be gratified through such a disordered activity as sneezing, while Eryximachus in return, warns him that his speech may not be taken seriously, if he jokes around like that.

Aristophanes', a comic playwright, reply comes in the form of a myth as he tells the tale of the three genders: male, female, and androgynous, all having four hands, four legs, two heads, two sets of genitals, and so on. They could move both forward and backward and ran by spinning themselves around in a cartwheel-like manner. Males were descended from the sun, females from the earth, while the androgynous descended from the moon. All were very powerful and made threatening attacks on the gods; however, the gods did not want to destroy them because in doing so they would forfeit the sacrifices humans made to them. Instead, Zeus decided to cut each person in two, while Apollo turned their heads around so that they would be facing toward the gash that had been made. Thus, they longed to return to their natural state, so people kept trying to find their other half to reunite with it. Eventually, Zeus took pity on them, and moved their genitals so they would be facing frontward, enabling them to have sexual intercourse. Those who were formerly androgynous could reproduce, and even two men who came together could at least have sexual satisfaction. This was the origin of our instinctive desire for affection, concern, and love for other human beings, declared Aristophanes. If Hephaestus, the blacksmith god, were to offer to weld a couple together so that they would become one and never be parted, even in death, they would leap at this opportunity. "Love" is the name that we give to our desire for wholeness, restoring ourselves to our original nature. Aristophanes observed that if we are disobedient or disorderly toward the gods, Zeus might split us in two once more, so we must always strive to behave and encourage others to behave well toward the gods.

Agathon, a playwright of tragedies, pointed out that all the previous speeches only spoke of the benefits that humans have gained from Love, but none had discussed the nature of the god himself. He suggested that Love is the happiest of the gods because he is most beautiful and best and that he is beautiful because, contrary to Phaedrus' claim, he is the youngest of the gods, always avoiding old age, and only associating with the young. Further, all the horrible things the gods did to each other in ancient times were due out of Necessity and not Love. However, since Love began ruling amongst the gods, everything was more peaceful. He suggested that Love is sensitive and settles in our minds and character and went on to speak about the virtues of Love, because he is never forced, nor uses force and everyone consents to his authority. Love practices moderation, since he can master pleasures and desires and Love is even braver than Ares, the god of war, since Ares fell in love with Aphrodite. He indicated that Love is wise since he is the inspiration for all other acts of wisdom and due to this no poet can be wise without Love, nor could the gods or muses master their respective arts without Love for those arts. He ended his oratory by adding that the gods only became organized when Love came into being, and thus, were motivated by a love of beauty.

After Agathon finished speaking, Socrates (who joined the group after his reverie on the porch) replied to him, "Bless you. How am I not going to be tongue-tied after a speech delivered with such beauty and variety?"[90] He begins by informing the group about his lack of prowess as a speaker, and in typical Socratic irony, pretends to know nothing about the nature of love, therefore throwing his fellow interlocutors off guard in order to teach them, for we know that Socrates was an excellent speaker! He begins by asking the host of the party, if he may ask him a few questions. "Is Love such as to be a love of something or of nothing?"[91] A father is father of his child. A brother is brother of his brother and sister. Is Love in like manner love of something? Love is of something that it lacks. If Love loves beauty; therefore it lacks beauty; therefore, it is not beautiful. Socrates points out the flaw in Agathon's argument: if love is beauty, then love desires beauty, and if love desires beauty, then it is lacking that quality, because we desire that which we lack. (In order to understand the *Symposium,* reflect back to previous references in this book, regarding the concept of Plato's theory of Forms where all the phenomena perceived by the senses are imitations of eternal perfections that alone have reality.)

Socrates introduced Diotima into the discussion, and reveals that as a youth; she taught him the philosophy of love. (Her ideas are the origin of the concept of Platonic love and her name means, "Honored by Zeus", and she was a philosopher, priestess or seer. There is debate whether Diotima was a real or fictional character invented by Plato. However, when we think about this, keep in mind that nearly all of the characters in the Platonic dialogues were real people living in ancient Athens.) He made the point that on one extreme, we have that which is good, fair, and beautiful, and at the other, we have that which is bad, foul, and ugly. He continued that, Love is neither a good nor a bad thing, therefore love is the "in between thing" for example, "in between" poverty and pleasure. Love is the means between wisdom and ignorance as well. No one who is already wise loves wisdom; and no one who is ignorant will love wisdom, because an ignorant person will not know that anything is lacking.[92] Diotima teaches, "Those who love wisdom fall in between those two extremes. And love is one of them, because he is in love with what is beautiful, and wisdom is extremely beautiful."[93] Love must be a lover of wisdom, therefore, love falls between being wise and being ignorant. What does love want? Love wants to possess some article of beauty. What do we get out of that? When we possess good things (Diotima substitutes "good" in place of beautiful to make her point), then we gain happiness; the goal in life is happiness. We are happy when we acquire good things, and we seek eternal happiness. She teaches that love (*Eros*) is the son of "resource and need", and it is the means of ascent to contemplation of the Divine. In Platonic love, the lovely or beautiful person will inspire the mind of the lover, and direct one's attention to spiritual things.

In Diotima's account of love, she talks about childbirth, its suffering, glory and beauty — a rare topic for the ancient Athenians. Her point is that we are all lovers who desire to create in a beautiful medium and to give birth in the beautiful. We are all pregnant to create, and to bring something to earth in a beautiful medium, needing to create something, which is eternal. We desire to leave behind a legacy of spiritual children. "First, it (love for the Form of Beauty) always is and neither comes to be nor passes away, neither waxes nor wanes. Second, it is not beautiful this way and ugly that way, nor beautiful at one time and ugly at another, nor beautiful in relation to one thing and ugly in relation to another; nor is it beautiful here but ugly there..." (Symposium 211a). The Form of the Beautiful is just what it is to be, "Beautiful itself, absolute, pure, unmixed, and not polluted by human flesh or colors or any other great nonsense of morality, but if he could see the divine Beauty itself in its one form." [94] Diotima teaches Socrates that the mystery of love leads us always upward for the sake of this one Beauty, and then to the consideration of Divinity, the source of Beauty, to the love of Divinity.[95] She explains to the young philosopher that love begins with the love of one beautiful soul or the attraction of one beautiful thing, and rises like a ladder to greater and greater generality and spirituality until one has the vision of the Beautiful itself. This rising of the human soul in perfection and love resonates with the modern student of spirituality; we open our hearts and souls to love one another, and as we develop a richer capacity to love, our own soul is enriched with this very beauty.

There were four primary Greek words to describe the concept of love: *eros, stergo, (storgo or astorgos), phileo,* and *agape.* The Greek word *eros* means a self-gratifying love, and it is focused on the individual and obtaining personal pleasure. *Eros* was a Greek term for sexual love, and it is where we get the word erotic. In the ancient Greek culture, this word referred to sensual, carnal impulses to gratify the sexual desires of the flesh. Our selfish love can grow into a social or Platonic Love, where we begin to consider others and temper our self-centered desires.

The Greek word *stergos* refers to the kind of love that comes naturally between family members; for example, the powerful love that a mother will experience when she gives birth to a child, or the love that a father has for his family, or the love that brothers and sisters have for one another. The Greek word *phileo* means brotherly love, or friendship. *Phileo* is a love based upon mutual satisfaction, and can feel disappointment, and can be the love and affection between two friends. This love is also based upon common interests, common goals, or personalities between two people who seem to get along well. There are numerous words derived from *phileo*, for example, Philadelphia (an ancient city in Lydia and a current city located in Pennsylvania, U.S.A.), a compound of *phileo,* and adelphos, which means brotherly love. *Philosophia* is another compound of *phileo* and *sophos*, which is the Greek word for wisdom. When these two words are compounded, they become philosophy, which means a love of wisdom. The word *agape* is a word whose meaning is filled with deep emotion and occurs when an individual sees, understands, or appreciates the value of a thing, object, or person, and holds this thing or person in great esteem, wonder or appreciation. Such a great attraction is awakened in the heart of the observer for what he or she is beholding that the observed person or object becomes irresistible. *Agape* love is a profound love that is limitless in its depth, height, and width. It is a self-sacrificial love that moves one to action. *Agape* love is a "no-strings" attached type, and it is not looking for what it can get, but for what it can give. This is a pure love; it is a love that is given even if there is no return. *Agape* love is the type of love that Socrates had for his fellow Athenians; he taught that if someone loved you, then they would love your soul.[96]

Socrates, a gifted speaker and teacher who never accepted money for imparting his wisdom, truly loved his fellow Athenians. The philosopher was often told that he should run for public office, but his inner voice advised him otherwise. Socrates believed that God ordered him to live his life as a philosopher and to examine himself and others, so that is what he did. For him, the highest purpose of love was to become a philosopher or a lover of wisdom and by doing so give birth to intellectual children (ideas) which will become immortal. In the *Symposium*, Socrates leaves the party and his fellow interlocutors asleep, and heads directly to the Lyceum where he washed up, and spent the rest of the day discussing the nature of the soul with his fellow Athenians. Do we know anyone like him today? What can we learn from him? What do you think about Platonic love?

CHAPTER THIRTEEN

God's Agape Love

Like a diamond embedded into the holy arc of angels, God's self-existence is cast in an eternal unchangeableness of light and love. We attempt to emulate this love in our own small way by loving others. In order to understand this devotion, we search for an objective certainty of our world, although both Christ and Socrates taught us that our perception of our world is actually uncertain. This doubt will not frighten us away from our development, because the mystery of God's intercession into our lives works to open our eyesight for a rare glimpse of the truth of love. The world will attempt to fool us away from Him, but we stand firm in our internal search for love, goodness, and being. In order to understand the highest agape love from God, we have examined the three lower forms: *eros, stergo, storgo* or *astorgos,* and *phileo.* Although agape love was not a common word in the ancient Greek speaking societies, it occurs 320 times in the New Testament to refer to

God's love for us, which is available through Christ who reconciles us to His Father.

We have learned that the Greek word *eros* means a self-gratifying love — it is focused on one's self, and what we can derive (often) in terms of pleasure. This word never appears in the New Testament, and its meaning is far removed from the type of love that believers aspire to in their marriage. Our selfish love can grow into a social love, where we begin to consider others and temper our self-centered desires. The Greek word *stergo* refers to the kind of love that comes naturally between family members and is a natural affection and good gift from God. "Husbands love your wives, just as Christ loved the Church and gave Himself up for her" (Eph 5:25). The use of *stergo* is rare in the New Testament; however, it is used in a negative sense in 2 Timothy, verse 3, where in the last days, the Apostle Paul tells us, "men will be unloving, irreconcilable, malicious gossips, without self-control, brutal, haters of good." The Apostle Paul is describing an evil so horrific that men will lack natural affection and devotion for members of their own family. He warns us that one of the principle signs of the last times will be the deterioration of the family and traditional family values. God has created us with natural affections for each other as members of our own families, and natural affections for members of our Christian kin. Paul teaches us in the end times, due to Satan, hearts will grow cold.

Our earlier examination of Plato's *Symposium* started us on our philosophical journey where we began to think about love — that wonderful force in nature that has served as the inspiration for poetry, songs, art, books, and the object of human desire. The prophetess Diotima taught Socrates the nature of love: we first ascend the ladder as a youth in adoration of the body. Then we capture the magnificence of soul and knowledge, which gives birth to the love of wisdom, wherein we eventually discover beauty itself. Love is the energetic force that drives all human activity, but always for the good and for the sake of happiness. The philosopher seeks love within the precepts of wisdom, wherein the philosophy of life teaches us to walk, work, stay and love within wisdom's light. Socrates was a man who loved his fellow Athenians, and he fervently taught them to care for their souls.

Platonic Greek philosophy merged with Christianity — first arising out of Judaism, and then flowing into the Biblical teaching of God's *agape* love. "You shall love the Lord your God with all your heart and with all your soul and with all your might" (Deut 6:5). Our freedom reveals itself as the movement of a free being in time; however, freedom must begin with our love for the Lord. "The aim of our charge is love that issues from a pure heart and a good conscience and sincere faith" (1 Tim 1:15). Our innate desire for freedom is our sensitivity toward being a whole man or woman, a human being who is completing him or herself in the Body of Christ. This freedom is always authentic and sets the pattern for a joy that will transfer to a clear and intuitive understanding of our gift from God. The sacred figure of Christ stands at the summit of our knowledge, and we awaken to the fact that everything that we have learned in this life was taught to us by our holy teacher, Christ and the Holy Spirit, in order that we would look inward for the beginning of our blessed life with Christ. God gives us symbols to enable us to understand His deep and profound mystery of love for us, and we examine these Biblical symbols, and replicate them in space-time. We understand God's Holy movements in a temporal-spatial sense, and use our reason, induction, knowledge, understanding, and spiritual intuition to construct — spatially — these holy symbols. We are spiritual beings — and fallen creatures — who live in a spatial-temporal world, and cannot overcome our identity within it, however we can keep our love, heart and mind on God.

"Love is patient, love is kind and is not jealous; love does not brag and is not arrogant, does not act unbecomingly; it does not seek its own, is not provoked, does not take into account a wrong suffered, does not rejoice in unrighteousness, but rejoices with the truth;" (1 Cor 13:4-6). Love binds the temporal and the eternal together — for God, time is nothing, however, our holy lessons are learned in the present. As we begin to understand God's *agape* love for us, we also learn to recognize what is authentic and real. Both Socrates and Christ taught from the known to the unknown; from particulars to universals; and from the simple to the complex idea. Socrates taught us the virtue of the soul; Christ taught us the way, truth and eternal life in Him. We are all on individual spiritual paths and experiencing a unique journey with the Lord. The Gospel teaches us to grow into our authentic selves by performing God's will: "You will know them by their fruits. Grapes are not gathered from thorn bushes nor figs from thistles, are they? So every good tree bears good fruit, but the bad tree bears bad fruit" (Mat 7:16-17). "Little children, let us not love with word or with tongue, but in deed and truth" (1 John 3:18).

God's governance of the universe is for moral ends, and He shapes and forms our moral character in the holy image of His son. Our tutelage in philosophy has assisted us on our spiritual journey — clarifying and defining abstract concepts that are God's map to the sanctification of our soul. His perfect love is meant to be actualized through our actions in life. The Apostle Paul taught us, "The love of God has been poured out within our hearts through the Holy Spirit who was given to us" (Rom 5:5).

God gives us knowledge of that which is good and the Bible teaches us to focus our thoughts on the positive, to know its true meaning (not as a contrast to what we see as evil), and to open our heart and soul to the manifestation of Him through His good works. Our actions are used as an instrument to testify to His love, truth and purity. The Apostle Paul taught us the nature of spiritual beauty, "I want you to be wise in what is good, and simple concerning evil" (Rom 16:19). Through God's *agape* love, all things are possible: we choose life, not death; we choose truth, not falsehood, and we choose love, not hate.

CHAPTER FOURTEEN

"The Lord is There"

The theory and art of induction — that we learned from Socrates — has taught us how to examine the Platonic *Dialogues,* and how to understand Socrates' teaching that "virtue is knowledge". Induction has assisted us as we examined Plato's *Republic,* learned the Allegory of the Cave, and the Platonic Theory of Forms. Like Socrates, Jesus' teaching was presented verbally, and we have applied the theory of induction to the Gospels that record the Good Word. We have used induction to examine the Four Gospels — Mathew, Mark, Luke and John — to shed light on the life and teaching of Jesus. The practice of induction led us as we studied the Bible and learned the particulars of God's Holy temples. We kept induction in mind as we thought about what makes up a spiritually good city. As we reflect upon Socrates' love for his fellow Athenians, and Jesus and God's *agape* love for us, we open our hearts so that this love may flow through us to others. The analytical power that we have learned from

Socrates has led us to think more deeply about our relationship to God and our spiritual mission.

We live in a secular time and are concerned with things in ordinary time, but as spiritual beings, we are also concerned with sacred time and eternity. For our understanding of the Holy Bible, events in the Old Testament can be linked as seemingly contiguous with events in the New Testament, even though the actual events have occurred centuries apart. For example, creation in Genesis in the Old Testament and the birth of our Lord Jesus in the New Testament are both sacred events that take place in secular time, and understanding the one event helps us to understand the other holy event, even though they are separated by many centuries. The events in the Old Testament that prefigure and herald our Savior reflect the New Testament order of worship and the New Covenant and the Holy Spirit. Plato wrote that reality or full being was outside of time in the realm of Ideas and was unchanging; what we see is changing and imperfect, and is an embodiment of the Ideas in time — a moving image of eternity. As Christians, we study the Bible and believe that God created the universe, "In the beginning God created the heavens and the earth. The earth was formless and void, and darkness was over the surface of the deep, and the Spirit of God was moving over the surface of the waters. Then God said, 'Let there be light' and there was light' " (Gn 1:1-3). God teaches us in time — all times are simultaneous for Him who holds the past, present and future in His sacred eternity. If we strive beyond our readiness for

God's promotion, it will lead to hubris and our downfall as Christians.

Acts is holy and edifying, but we will take Book 1 to initiate us in the inductive methodology of studying the Bible. John the Baptist prophesized that he baptized with water but Christ would baptize with the Holy Spirit (Mat 3:11, Mark 1:8, Luke 3:16, and John 1:33). Jesus appeared to His disciples after His suffering on the cross, and His resurrection, and He stayed with them... over a period of forty days and spoke to them about the kingdom of God. "Do not leave Jerusalem, but wait for the gift my Father promised, which you have heard me speak about. For John was baptized with water, but in a few days you will be baptized with the Holy Spirit" (Acts 1:3-5). We review our inductive questions, and ask, 'what' were the disciples promised? They were promised the gifts of the Holy Spirit. The question 'when', is answered when we read in Acts 2 that the gifts of the Holy Spirit came upon the disciples, "When the day of the Pentecost came, they were all together in one place" (Acts 2:2). This also answers the 'where'; they were in Jerusalem. The question 'what occurred' is answered here; "Suddenly a sound like the blowing of a violent wind came from heaven and filled the whole house where they were sitting. They saw what seemed to be tongues of fire that separated and came to rest on each of them. All of them were filled with the Holy Spirit and began to speak in other tongues as the Spirit enabled them" (Acts 2:3-4). The 'why' is answered because the event fulfilled the prophecies that spoke of the last days and that the Spirit would be imparted (Isa 32:15; and

Joel 2:28-32). The coming of the Spirit marked the beginning of the church, and the presence of the Holy Spirit fulfilled Jesus' promise to His disciples that He would not leave them orphaned. The presence of the Holy Spirit gave the disciples the power to proclaim the Gospel throughout the region with the empowering presence of God.

The following examples are presented in the book of Acts: the stoning of Stephen (7:54-60), Saul's conversion (9:22-23), Peter's vision (10:9-13), Peter's visit to the home of Cornelius (that was directed by the Holy Spirit and where the Holy Spirit was poured upon the Gentiles) (10:44-46), Paul's (Saul's) missionary journey (13). In the church at Antioch, the prophets and teachers were praying, fasting and worshiping the Lord, when the Holy Spirit said, "Set apart for me Barnabas and Saul for the work to which I have called them" (Acts 13:1-3). Paul believed that we are the temples of the Holy Spirit, and the through it, our Lord lives on in us. The sequence of events in Paul's life after his conversion are voiced in Acts where we learn that he made several major missionary journeys from Antioch to Jerusalem, to Corinth, to Ephesus, to Jerusalem again, to Caesarea, and then to Rome where he is indicted and imprisoned for two years (Acts 28:16-31). "God did extraordinary miracles through Paul. Handkerchiefs and aprons that had touched him were taken to the sick, and their illnesses were cured and the evil spirits left them" (Acts 19:11-12). Throughout the book of Acts, people pray and God responds to their prayers. Paul was obedient to God's mission that directed him to spread the Holy Word throughout the ancient kingdoms (he even went to Athens); and he was energetic, steadfast, humble, and a vessel for God's Divine work.

The Cross of Jesus Christ stands as a holy reminder to us of our redemption and the Lord's love for us. His cross is at the center of our time, and is positioned at the apex of our space — as a pivotal and sacred moment in eternity. In this humble Christian endeavor, we have applied the principles of induction to align our Christian knowledge in the light of the Lord's perfect wisdom. "Wait on the Lord" (Psalms 27:14); our activities are centered on the platform of our Lord. We pray for redemption and access into the Holiest Realm; the spirit of God's Holy Ark is within our heart. "Be anxious for nothing, but in everything by prayer and supplication, with thanksgiving, let your requests be made known to God" (Phil 4:6). "Therefore, brethren, having boldness to enter the Holiest by the blood of Jesus" (Heb 10:19). Consequently, I will strike boldly and petition the Lord: This is my fervent prayer and supplication for the children of God. I pray that His spirit of Christian freedom blesses the face of the earth. A covenant of hope and desire and love for the Lord will bind this material world to the spiritual for an embodiment of freedom on this noble planet. Amen. "He stretches out the north over empty space, and hangs the earth on nothing" (Job 26:7). Human beings have always desired to be free and our souls are innately spiritual; so we pursue those things that bring us comfort, joy, peace, and happiness. We are adept at achieving material things, and can shape and reshape our world for our pleasure, and now we have matured in our appreciation of what gives us true happiness. The exercise of the ideas of freedom in Christ will strengthen our soul's capacity and ability to achieve true freedom in Him.

Through inductive methodology and analytical power, we examined the Old and New Testament, the Tabernacle of Moses, The Temple of David, and the Temple of Solomon. In our studies, we have probed the specific structures within the sites, construction, priests, chambers, symbolism of the material used, and the particular colors. The same Ark of the Lord occupied all three holy structures with the Shekinah Glory-Fire of the Lord. In Exodus, Moses completes the Tabernacle according to God's instructions, "Then the cloud covered the tent of meeting, and the glory of the Lord filled the Tabernacle. Moses was not able to enter the tent of meeting because the cloud had settled on it, and the glory of the Lord filled the tabernacle" (Ex 40:34-35). God gave Ezekiel a vision of a new Temple, where the Shekinah Glory of the Lord will return and dwell in His place in the City, forever. "Then he led me to the gate, the gate facing toward the east; and behold, the glory of the God of Israel was coming from the way of the east. And His voice was like the sound of many waters; and the earth shone with His glory" (Ez 43:1-2). "The city shall be 18,000 cubits round about; and the name of the city from that day shall be, 'The Lord is there' " (Ez 48:35).

As a nation, we have outgrown our youth and now, mature, we want to claim our heritage — freedom in Christ. No one can take that heritage away from us! Our national birthright is a Christian nation, where our belief in One Holy God remains our foundation and our blessing. Our individual birthright is one of individual freedom in Jesus Christ, and our natural endowment and desire is to live in a free Christian nation. We exercise this fulfillment in matter and material objects as a spiritual activity that will strengthen the soul's capacity for freedom in Him.

The fundamental spiritual ideas of freedom become easier to visualize if we examine each dimension in Christ: freedom of self (width and length), freedom of the intellect (breadth), freedom of movement (temporal), and freedom of ratiocination/reasoning (spatial). Our desire for freedom in Christ is our spiritual drive — becoming a whole man or woman in Him. Our freedom reveals itself as the movements of an autonomous being in time, and we utilize our reason to construct our ideas spatially. How can we feel secure in developing a relationship to perfect things in another dimension, (for our God is not bound by space or time), when our classroom is situated in the here and now? The answer to this question is in a realm of faith that is strengthened as we study and utilize our inductive methodology and analytical skills to focus on the Holy Bible.

We have demonstrated the process of Christian ratiocination with the use of inductive methodology for a study and understanding of the Holy Bible. While our Lord was on earth, his body was confined to the human limitations of time and space, but His Holy Spirit was atemporal and aspatial. Our ascended Lord is the fullness of the Godhead bodily. When we are in Christ, we partake of a measure of the fullness therein, with the

Grace of God, while we are confined to the limitations of time and space. Paul penned the Glory of the mystery of the Lord, "We proclaim Him, admonishing every man and teaching every man with all wisdom, so that we may present every man complete in Christ. For this purpose also I labor, striving according to His power, which mightily works within me" (Col 1: 28-29). "But we speak God's wisdom in a mystery, the hidden wisdom which God predestined before the ages to our glory" (1 Cor 2:7). We have learned from our theory and practice of induction that the Christian precepts are teachable patterns that will assist us in our development for a freedom of self in Christ; Christ trains us for reigning with Him and these teachable patterns will support our spiritual growth. The Lord teaches us these archetypes through His Holy Word, for example, The Tabernacle of Moses, The Temple of David, The Temple of Solomon, The Second Temple, The New Testament Church, and New Jerusalem. These spiritual patterns are our Christian heritage, and they will assist us in forming the righteous and special habits that are required of us to be holy in the sight of our Lord.

In the age of freedom in Christ, we are independent, applying the knowledge gained from the sound and spiritual ideas of past Christian thinkers. The precise questions of induction that we have employed in our intimate and holy study of the Holy Bible yield further questions: what predominant spiritual ideas are the foundations for our freedom in Christ? Which ideas take precedence over other ideas, and how can we be more holy through this practice? What Christian ideas of will we use to ensure the development of a free nation? What ideas of freedom are true to our Christian precepts as taught to us by Him? What concepts of freedom will advance our goal of an expanded individual freedom for ourselves and for others? What thoughts stimulate our intellect and feed our souls? For guidance in our search for answers, we pray for the Holy Spirit to enlighten us with wisdom both in theory and in practice. We boldly go forward with Christ's guidance, and pray for wisdom to understand and communicate the spiritual ideas that have been taught to us by the Holy Spirit. Paul taught us, "Not that I have already obtained it or have already become perfect, but I press on so that I may lay hold of that for which also I was laid hold of by Christ Jesus" (Phil 3:12). "Brethren, join in following my example, and observe those who walk according to the pattern you have in us" (Phil 3:17). We pray that the saints may guide us, as we follow a sound and holy Christian religion as a disciple of Christ.

The exploration of any new Christian territory is at the same time both exhilarating and uncomfortable. We can feel that we have been cast ashore onto a strange land, but a continued intellectual exploration of the new territory will reveal that what at first appeared to be very alien may in fact have some spatial aspects that are familiar to us. We can map the unfamiliar idea onto our logical thinking in order to stretch our imagination. Discussion, examination, and reexamination lead to a dynamism that keeps our intellect alive: while God feeds our heart and soul, and expands our understanding. Our intellect and creative energy will carry us forward to analyze and understand the precepts, commandments, ideas and concepts that God has taught us through His Holy Word, "For you were called to freedom, brethren; only do not turn your freedom into an opportunity for the flesh, but through love serve one another" (Gal 5:13). Our human nature is innately a freedom-loving one so those ideas will assist us in presenting a model for our freedom in Christ.

We are born to be free, and when Christ presents us to God, this freedom is redeemed for He is our Holy Mediator. We know when Christ is calling us because there is a holy and irresistible power that draws us to His Heart. The idea of freedom in Christ is teachable on an individual level. The reality of Christianity becomes substantial and workable when it arises from within the receptacle of individuality, and we follow the Lord's instructions with prayer and good works within the Church — the body of Christ. The good works of the spirit also embrace the community where families live and work. These centers, as a whole, are the guardians for the nation's health in Christ. Individual freedom is not theoretical dogma but is an active force when the replication of the holy idea of the Christian is one who is moving and living in Him. As we pray to our Lord, "At the acceptable time I listened to you, and on the day of salvation I helped you. Behold, now is the 'acceptable time,' behold now is 'the day of the Salvation' " (2 Cor 6:2).

The concept of freedom resonates in the intellect of each individual, and the principle of freedom is extended in a societal class. Each individual has a unique function in Christ, as does the Church, and the community as a whole; they are similar in the end toward which they seek, varying in degree but not in kind: to build the New Testament Church and individual salvation, and to worship, love, and glorify the Lord. This glorious end is the maximum Christian freedom that the individual strives for — living blessed within our Lord. To maintain our Christian heritage of salvation and freedom, and to achieve the goal of the New Testament Church, we will obey the Lord's commandments, and adhere to Christian ethics. An individual obedient to Christ's Word is an individual animated in morality and spirit, and in turn, this person will assist in activating a good Church and community. "Or do you not know that your body is a temple of the Holy Spirit who is in you, whom you have from God, and that you are not your own? For you have been bought with a price: therefore glorify God in your body" (1 Cor 6:19-20). This moral, mental and heartfelt concordance, as taught to us by Christ, and preached by the Apostle Paul, will nurture a future generation of gifted, free, and independent wisdom seekers, who will adhere to the precept that an individual is spiritually activated through the spirit of our Lord.

"Take My yoke upon you and learn from Me, for I am gentle and humble in heart, and you will find rest for your souls. For my yoke is easy and My burden is light" (Mat 11:29-30). Jesus summons us so that we may envision an eternal life as inheritors of the Kingdom. The spatial configuration of such a community will matter in order that we can draft a design that will be in harmony with the figure of a moral Christianity, i.e., to architecturally mimic to the highest degree possible that which is holy, beautiful, and good in form and function. With God's guidance, the citizens are the developers of this design and pattern, and they work together in order to build the Christian city. The citizens of this community are the best of natures and will remain sound in mind, active in Christian morality, and practicing in their function in Christ: "in the hope of eternal life, which God, who cannot lie, promised long ages ago" (Titus 1:2).

God teaches us that His commandments and Holy Word must be exercised as a practical responsibility within our family and marriage, Church, community, friendships, and nation; we relate and apply the God-breathed Gospel in our good works as Christians. For example, as a Christian nation we express God's goodness in form, i.e., in our Constitution, as an idea of freedom and equality. These are ideas from our teaching in the Lord. However, the powers of a democracy acquire a maximum force through the activity of the citizens not just through an idea. It is not only essential that the government (sanctioned by the Constitution), as the form of the community, allocates and distributes power as required by the law, but it is also necessary that the material, i.e., the citizens, also fulfill their individual functions and vocation as the electors of this representative democracy. The citizens are the ideational masters that feed the original form in order to enliven its function and capabilities, and this implies a strengthening (not an enlargement, as we have today!) of the fundamental form.

As we follow Christian philosophy and study the Word of God, we believe that freedom is a concept that will continue to thrive. Our intellect rests on a substructure of life: the freedom of the mind rests on a substructure of being; the freedom of the soul rests on a substructure of spirit, so the imperative maxim for a democratic community is that form which supports the foundation for individual freedom: this form is Christ, and the foundation is the New Testament Church. Freedom for the individual was purchased through the Blood of Christ; therefore, He has assured His believers of everlasting salvation. This community in itself can only represent the qualities that are reflected by each individual Christian in his or her walk with the Lord. If the individuals lead by good example by exhibiting Christian brotherly love, then we have a community that reflects the covenant relationship that God commanded us to develop for His Church. The conception of the community as an isolated entity is false; a community is an association of God-fearing and active individuals who gain a social momentum through Christian ideas, education in the Word, practical learning, and active participation as good citizens. Paul, a bondservant of Christ Jesus said, "Be devoted to one another in brotherly love; give preference to one another in honor" (Rom 12:10). The dignity of the citizen begins with his or her movement in the Lord and a fervent desire to understand God's wisdom and laws for us. A person who aspires toward holy wisdom is also a person of deep and abounding faith, and this faith is always based upon spiritual health. The Apostle Paul taught us, "Be of the same mind toward one another; do not be haughty in mind, but associate with the lowly. Do not be wise in your own estimation" (Rom 12:16). If we take a foothold in our city from our own unshakeable belief in God, then from this frame of reference we will gain a bold confidence to participate in our Church, community, and government. This faith connection between The New Testament Church, individual citizens, community, and the government is mutually beneficial because it affirms that — through the grace of God — we can acquire individual happiness and fulfillment in the Lord and at the same time seek a stability of existence and freedom for our community. The problems that arise in a civilized society are solvable, and each solution leads to a further clarification of the magnitude of freedom, and a further specification of what it means to be free in Christ. Christian freedom evolves as we actively participate as citizens of our Church and community; a work of spiritual freedom entails work toward the Creator's Holy freedom for us in the Body of Christ. Paul reminds us, "By common confession, great is the mystery of godliness: He who was revealed in the flesh, Was vindicated in the Spirit, Seen by angels, Proclaimed among the nations, Believed on in the world, Taken up in Glory" (1 Tim 3:9).

God guides us in our development of His Word and He protects our soul from evil for the edification of His Kingdom. We are the earthly hands for the building of The New Testament Church — a holy place of worship that we call the City of God. God's city exists; we have the idea clearly in mind, and as God has revealed each aspect of His Holy City to us, the whole pattern becomes illuminated by God's Holy Word. We become sensitive to the areas that we personally need to develop as we grow within our own relationship to Him. "There is a river whose streams make glad the city of God, the holy dwelling places of the Most High. God is in the midst of her, she will not be moved" (Psalms 46:4-5). Christian activity is the key to create this City: our spiritual energy of obedience, faith, and a deep trust of God's truth that we apply in our everyday walk with the Lord. "Offer the sacrifices of righteousness, And trust in the Lord" (Psalms 4:5). It is not the work that we personally perform in the service of the Lord, but the work that God does through us. Each individual member is remarkable in his Christ-like constitution, yet more extraordinary is the composition of the Holy Body of Christ and the Holy Church of God. We all experience our share of sorrows in life and pray when we hear of misfortune that befalls others, and evil acts seem to be more prevalent today than in the past. We pray for forgiveness of our transgressions, and for God's forgiveness of our fellow human beings. We are all in the world together as we turn toward the light, make progress, and then often suffer setbacks. We renew our spiritual health within a good community.

Our holy blueprint for the New Testament Church found in the Holy Bible is the inspired Words of God written down and preserved through the centuries for our knowledge, understanding, and edification of the Lord. We are animated with the essence of His vision for us, so we raise ourselves up with a joyful zeal for the job at hand. We pray to the Lord for eyes to see and ears to hear, so that we may be in harmony with God's mission for us. Our labor of love is to create a Church following the pattern that God has commanded for His Temple. Nebuchadnezzar destroyed the Temple of Jerusalem in 586 B.C., however, there would be another Temple, and another Jerusalem that would be called *Jehovah-shammah*, the Lord is there! This temple in the New Jerusalem is where the Lord will dwell forever. Ezekiel had a vision, "Then he led me to the gate facing toward the east; and behold; the glory of the God of Israel was coming from the way of the east. And His voice was like the sound of many waters; and the earth shone with His glory ...and the name of the city from that day shall be, 'The Lord is there' " (Ez 43:43; 48:35).

The Church is composed of individuals whose minds and hearts focus on spiritual growth in the Lord; in this light, we do not lose sight of the importance of the objective world as the workshop for our spirituality. It is not a collective, nor is it an intermediate step to our personal achievements; building the Church is the goal as each person creates though their own spiritual gifts. The sensitive and complex person can suffer from the brutality in the world; therefore, we pray to inhabit a city without decadence. The ancient apostolic spirit is alive and a gift within the walls of the City, and here we witness a transfiguration from active human beings to activity of the spirit on the highest level. Our beautiful City is built in the valley by the shadow of the most majestic mountain and protected by the warm and life-giving waters of the ocean. God's soldiers create and achieve a heavenly place within His walls through the mystery and depth of God's love for us.

The Christian philosopher's *gnosis* develops *arête* toward the earthly city, which is the shadow of the heavenly City. We join the two worlds together through our love for God; and it is love that we reflect when we devote ourselves in labor for the development of His Church. The division of the earthly and heavenly Church is in reality the division of mind and heart; and the healing hand of the Lord will heal this schism. Jesus taught at the Synagogue quoting the prophet Isaiah: "The Spirit of the Lord is upon Me, because He has sent Me to proclaim release to the captives, and recovery of sight to the blind, to set free those who are oppressed, to proclaim the favorable year of the Lord" (Luke 4:18). Our spiritual self-determination strengthens through the Lord who is our balm for curing the disease of separation from our Father. Luke writes in Acts that believers were healed through the hands of the apostles, "to such an extent that they even carried the sick out into the streets and laid them on cots and pallets, so that when Peter came by at least his shadow might fall on any one of them" (Acts 5:15). Our healing in Christ is the pattern of *gnosis* and the Holy Spirit lays out this map, so that we may take heart and have courage to travel His way through our own spiritual development. God's foreordination and foreknowledge does not preclude our freedom in Christ, because freedom is the attainment of a pure being in God's Holy image. What appears to be causal determination is in fact the initiative of the free will of our actions. It is difficult to progress in the holy growth that is spiritually important, because we generally do not receive an instant reward, praise, or recognition by our fellow humans (and most often, we do not ourselves understand the holiness of our current development). "The angel of the Lord encamps around those who fear Him, and rescues them. O taste and see that the Lord is good; how blessed is the man who takes refuge in Him!" (Psalms 34:7-8).

Our inductive methodology is a logical framework for the intellect to proceed through symbols, signs and concepts, and this method strengthens our faculties for the perception of the archetypes of God. Socrates has taught us how to use our logical framework to understand and recognize archetypes, and our Lord has taught us how God's precepts are illuminated to us through Christian activity in conjunction with prayerfulness. Our Christian gifts and giftedness of soul leads to our purity of thought in Christ. God's archetypes are holy shields that protect us, His creatures, from the fiery countenance of God. God's archetypes and symbols illuminate us, and protect us from a spiritual intensity that we are not yet prepared to comprehend. If we can remain humble in the light of accolades for our accomplishments (and remember that it is the echo of God's whispering that we anxiously wait, and His movement that we faithfully follow), then we will be part of the glory of His inheritance. In pure Newtonian fashion, we show our scientific face to agnostics while turning our face ever more often to the light. The transcendence of space, time, and ordinary knowledge into the spiritual realm requires total concentration of the mind, heart, and soul.

We are culturally conditioned to perceive the material world, so as God's children, it is our spiritual obligation to break through this barrier and to live spiritually in the light. God and His saints will nurse us back to health as He uses the external, material world to bring about internal purification for His followers.

Our aspiration as Christians is to separate ourselves away from evil and anchor ourselves in God's good. The unbroken story from the ancient Biblical era where we learned about the patriarchs of Israel, to ancient Greece and Socrates where we learned our inductive logic, to the first-century Biblical era and the birth and teaching of our beloved Christ, to modernity, and the computer age, we continually hold fast to His commandments. God created Adam and Eve to have an intimate relationship with Him, as well as all their descendants, and through our worship and in our Christian metaphysics, we exist and thrive in our rapport with God. The Holy Spirit is present in our lives, praise the Lord! In our Christian ethics, we behave morally as God's children of light. In our epistemology, we strive for the true knowledge of God. We want to know God through personal and divine revelation; we pray for redemption through His Holy Son. We keep in mind that often God wants us to unlearn something, "Your ears will hear a word behind you, This is the way, walk in it, whenever you turn to the right or to the left" (Isa 30:21). Our worship and love for God is divine, and is the love of a Christian child for our Holy Father.

As Christians, we all have opinions, beliefs, faith, and trust, and seek the truth in the Lord. Our way of thinking is not just an abstraction but also a way of life, where our high expectations and aspirations set goals for our family and ourselves. Christians are committed to discerning God's truth and we will act on this truth, searching for the perfection of the soul. In God's city, we band together for the pursuit of His wisdom, and in this new city, we each bear a good conscience for that which is good. We look for the intelligible light found within a pure Christ conscience. We can envision a future, and learn from the past that it is God's wisdom, not our wisdom, that will create a free city. As His creatures, we are destined and fit for existence in a free community, where we have in mind the form of that which is good and a heart of love for God. Christianity has prepared us for freedom with our self-determination and extensive action in the Lord, and the authenticity of a loving God. Apostle Paul teaches, "For you were called to freedom, brethren; only do not turn your freedom into an opportunity for the flesh but through love serve one another" (Gal 5:13).

"O Lord, You have searched me and know me" (Psalms 139:1). Our study of Christian symbols, signs, and inductive logic is for our knowledge and understanding of the Word, but these concepts alone do not nourish us on our deepest spiritual level; we desire to know the divine thing itself. Contemplation of the most sacred things in life leads to a pure meditation upon God's goodness, where we learn to honor the soul, which further leads us to a deeper love and worship of God. "Let my meditation be pleasing to Him; As for me, I shall be glad in the Lord" (Psalms 104:34). Meditation does not lead to an ascetic way of life, but to an active Christian one, where we develop the ideas taught by the Lord. God's New Testament Church is where the inhabitants are free, enlightened, and happy, and the admirable qualities found naturally in the Christian soul are activated and visible in physical actions. We anticipate building the New Temple Church where the saying, "brotherly love" is more than just a slogan. Our effective life is in spirit and spirit is in God, and His grace toward us makes us beautiful in heart and soul. "You are fairer than the sons of me; Grace is poured upon Your lips; Therefore God has blessed You forever" (Psalms 45:2). The labors of the mind are to feed the Spirit, where the supreme counselor of the intellect is the Holy Spirit. "Make me know Your ways, O Lord; Teach me Your paths. Lead me in Your truth and teach me. For You are the God of my salvation; For You I wait all the day" (Psalms 25:4-5).

We find the first mention of the New Testament Church in the Gospel of Mathew when Jesus said, "I also say to you that you are Peter, and upon this rock I will build My Church; and the gates of Hades will not overpower it" (Mat 16:18). Jesus was referring to the spiritual Church made up of all believers with the spiritual body of Christ as the head. All of the apostles are the foundation of the New Testament Church; Peter was the first living stone to make his confession of faith to the Lord. After Paul's conversion on the road to Damascus, he said of Jesus, "He is the son of God" (Acts 9:20). Paul teaches us in Romans, "that if you confess with your mouth Jesus as Lord, and believe in your heart that

God raised Him from the dead, you will be saved; for with the heart a person believes, resulting in righteousness, and with the mouth he confesses, resulting in salvation" (Rom 10:9-10). This heavenly Church is eternal and still in the process of construction. Our use of language, for example, building, construction, and labor is the same terminology that was used in the construction of the Old Testament and the New Testament Church, and this language allows us to focus on our ministry in the Lord. Our love and service to God equips us for functioning where He has placed us. Christ is our rock foundation for the New Testament Church. Jesus tells Peter, "I will give you the keys of the kingdom of heaven; and whatever you bind on earth shall have been bound in heaven, and whatever you loose on earth shall have been loosed in heaven" (Mat 16:19). Jesus entrusts The New Testament Church to administer the Kingdom of God on the earth.

We seek God's kingdom through our identification with His seat of authority on earth in the New Testament Church. Jesus taught, "But seek first His kingdom and His righteousness, and all these things will be added to you. Therefore, do not worry about tomorrow for tomorrow will take care of itself. Each day has enough trouble of its own" (Mat 6:33-34). We oftentimes think about George Washington, who — wearing his Masonic apron — set the cornerstone for our Capital, symbolizing the solid foundation for our nation of freedom under God. His children of light will gather the stones for building His Holy Church, and will lay the most holy of stones for the foundation. He beckons His children, so let us assist in the construction of our Father's Church, so others will follow and take up residence in His house. Although we are humbly aware that it is God's providence, we feel in our heart that He will call Socrates, Aristotle, Plato, Saint Joan of Arc, Saint Francis, and all of the saints and apostles to dwell in His heavenly abode.

God's Holy New Testament Church has members who belong to the association of freedom in Christ, and this freedom is created through our active participation, drawing its substantiality from the ensuing spirituality. Freedom in Christ cannot change its truth-value, nor can it cease to exist; what is variable about His Holy freedom is human participation. The beauty of Christian freedom is that it is universal and yet individual — universal in the Body of Christ, and individual when it expresses the very best qualities of holiness that men and women can achieve. Our singular lives are variable and can bring different challenges to everyone, but the value of freedom in Him remains constant and Holy. God presents us with unique challenges and problems where we are able to discern the truth in objects, things, and circumstances — the solution to these problems is through holy growth of the self in Christ. This initiation is the revelation of the free self, and is the stimulation for us to move closer toward freedom in Him.

Socrates anticipates Christian ethics of goodness and morality, and we have learned from him that "virtue is knowledge." We have studied the ancient Greeks with their worship for gods and spirits, and admired Plato's *Republic* where the inhabitants develop their tripartite souls in order to achieve the most harmonious of cities possible. We have learned from both Socrates and Jesus how to develop our inductive methodology in order to better understand ourselves, and as Christians, we learn our mission appointed to us by our Sacred and Holy God. In summary, we have utilized Socratic inductive methodology to study Socratic and Platonic philosophy as a starting exercise to practice our reasoning powers. We have applied this same inductive methodology to the study of the Holy Bible with the goal of increasing our intimacy with the Word of God. We have studied the Old and New Testaments, and applied our inductive questions — where, who, when, how, why and what — to our analysis and interpretation of the Holy Word. We have also asked the questions: what happened over the span of time, and how do the people, places, and things relate to one another in space. Our goal was to see, observe, understand, interpret, and apply the Holy Word to our lives as Christians. God is our appointed teacher in the study of His Holy Word, and as we love, worship, trust, obey, and grow in the Body of Christ, we achieve these objectives, for His *agape* love for us has opened our minds and hearts with the essence of Christianity.

United under the belief of one God and His Holy Son, Jesus Christ, and with a clear religious voice, we proclaim the living Word of God. His free love covers all of humanity, and is not limited to a select group of religious believers. The fountainhead of religious freedom in Christ is the wholesome and unrestricted *agape* love of God flowing through our hearts and souls, and through the community. The Temple of God is truly in each Christian heart and in each Christian home within

God's City. Love is always accompanied by desire, and this longing for the Lord inspires us to work in harmony laying the beautiful bricks of the New Jerusalem. We are ready to construct God's Temple and we pray for the fulfillment of the City of Light. Through our love of the Lord, we remain submissive as workers in this City, obedient and fearful of His power and judgment, obedient to His commandments, struck by His majesty and Beauty, and worshipful to His glory. The child of God is a child of the City of God; we look to Him and in this vision, we desire to mature our soul with His precepts. The votaries of the City of God are bound by their love in common to the Holy *Elohim*. "Then I saw a new heaven and a new earth; for the first heaven and the first earth passed away, and there is no longer any sea. And I saw the holy city, New Jerusalem, coming down out of heaven from God, made ready as a bride adorned for her husband. And I heard a loud voice from the throne saying, 'Behold, the tabernacle of God is among men, and He will dwell among them, and they shall be His people, and God Himself will be among them'" (Rev 21:1-3).

The child born under the stars, sun and moon, and nourished by Our Lady, is held up to Heaven — immortality for that sweet Prince of God. We pray, earnestly and humbly, for the blessings of peace for our earth and her inhabitants, so that we may return to Him: holy, pure, well, and sound, so that God may bless us and that we may live up to His blessings.

254 · Joan Arnsteen

MEET THE AUTHOR

JOAN ARNSTEEN HOLDS A DOCTOR OF RELIGIOUS EDUCATION DEGREE FROM DESTINY UNIVERSITY, A MASTER'S DEGREE IN CONSTITUTIONAL HISTORY FROM WAYNE STATE UNIVERSITY, AND AN UNDERGRADUATE DEGREE IN PHILOSOPHY. THE AUTHOR CAN BE REACHED AT HER BLOG AT SOCRATESPLACE.COM.

REFERENCES

Augustine of Hippo. The City of God, translated by Henry Bettenson, Harmondsworth, England, Penguin Classics, 2003.

Bible: The New Inductive Study Bible. Eugene, Oregon: Precept Ministries International, Harvest House Publishers, 2000.

Brickhouse, Thomas C. and Smith, Nicholas D. *Plato's Socrates.* New York: Oxford University Press, 1994.

Colaiaco, James. *Why Socrates Died.* London: Routledge, 2001.

Conner, Kevin J. *The Tabernacle of Moses.* Portland, Oregon: City Christian Publishing, 1988.

Cooper, John M., ed. *Plato Complete Works.* Indianapolis, Cambridge: Hackett Publishing Co., 1997.

Goldstein, Rebecca Newberger. *Plato at the Googleplex.* New York: Pantheon Books, 2014.

Homer. *The Iliad,* translated by Robert Fagles. New York: Penguin Books, 1990.

Homer. *The Odyssey,* translated by Robert Fagles. New York: Penguin Books, 1996.

Hendricks, Howard G. and Hendricks, William D. *Living by the Book.* Chicago: Moody Publishers, 2007.

Hughes, Bettany. *The Hemlock Cup.* New York: Vintage Books, 2012.

Irwin, Terence. *Plato's Ethics.* New York and Oxford: Oxford University Press, 1995.

McKeon, Richard, ed. *The Basic Works of Aristotle*. New York: Random House, 1941.

Nails, Debra. *The People of Plato, A Prosopography of Plato and Other Socratics*. Indianapolis, IN: Hackett Publishing Co., 2002.

Priestley, Joseph. *Jesus and Socrates Compared*. Kessinger Legacy Reprints originally published 1803.

Scodel, Ruth. *Sophocles*. Boston: Twayne Publishers, 1984.

Segal, Erich, ed. *Oxford Readings in Aristophanes*. New York: Oxford University Press, 1996.

Sharansky, Natan. *The Case for Democracy: The Power of Freedom to Overcome Tyranny & Terror*. New York: Public Affairs, 2004

Strassler, Robert, ed. *The Landmark Thucydides*. New York: Simon & Shuster, 1996.

Tabor, James D. *The Jesus Dynasty*. New York: Simon & Shuster, 2006.

Taylor, A.E. *Plato: The Man and His Work*. London: Methuen, 1926.

Taylor, Walter F. Jr. *Paul Apostle to the Nations*. Minneapolis: Fortress Press, 2012.

Vlastos, Gregory. *Socrates: Ironist and Moral Philosopher*. Ithaca, NY: Cornell University Press, 1991.

Waterfield, Robin. *Why Socrates Died. Dispelling the Myths*. New York: W.W. Norton & Company, 2009.

Wenham, G.J., Motyer, J.A., Carson, D. A., and France, R. T., eds. *The New Bible Commentary*. Downers Grove, IL: Intervarsity Press, 2010.

Xenophon: Conversations of Socrates, translated by Hugh Tredennick and Robin Waterfield. New York: Penguin Books, 1990.

1	All scripture quotations are taken from The New Inductive Study Bible version unless otherwise noted, Precept Ministries International, Harvest House Publishers, 2000.
2	Plato, *Plato: Complete Works, Apology* 42a3-4, ed. John M. Cooper, Indianapolis/Cambridge, Hackett Publishing Co. 1997
3	There are numerous attributes of God including holiness, aseity, graciousness, immanence, immutability, incorporeity, mission, mystery, oneness, providence, sovereignty, transcendence, and veracity. This enumeration of God's attributes is not an inclusive list – "God is spirit" (John 4:24).
4	Plato, *Plato: Complete Works,* Republic II, 361e2-3-362a1.
5	Ibid. *Meno*, 77e
6	Ibid. *Meno* 81c4-d5
7	We also learn about Socrates from the writings of Xenophon, Aristotle, and Aristophanes.
8	Plato, *Plato: Complete Works, Phaedrus,* 249a1-5
9	Thucydides, *History of the Peloponnesian War*, trans. R. Warner, London, Penguin Books, 1972. 2.34-2.46.
10	Plato, *Menexenus,* 236a.
11	Plato, *Menexenus,* 236d4-249d.
12	Ibid. *Symposium*, 220e1-2.
13	Nails, Debra, *The People of Plato*, p. 17-20.

14	Plato, *Plato: Complete Works, Apology*, 32 d1-e 2.
15	Ibid. *Alcibiades*, 130e6-7.
16	Ibid. *Gorgias* 448d9-10.
17	Ibid. *Apology*, 38a1-6.
18	Ibid. *Apology*, 29e1-2.
19	Ibid. see the *Symposium*.
20	Ibid. *Republic X*, 617b3-c 2.
21	Ibid. *Apology*, 38b11.
22	Ibid. *Apology*, 41d1-2.
23	Ibid. *Phaed*, 59b8.
24	Ibid. *Republic V*, 475-480.
25	Ibid. *Apology*, 38a1-2.
26	Ibid. *Apology*, 29d 6-7; 29e 1-3.
27	Ibid. *Meno*, 71a, 100b.
28	Ibid. *Phaedrus*, 279b8-c 4.
29	Ibid. *Craytlus*, 407b.
30	Ibid. *Timaeus*, 24c-d.
31	Ibid. *Republic VII*, 514a-b.
32	Ibid. *Republic VII,* 532c.
33	Ibid. *Republic VII*, 514b-532c.
34	Ibid. *Republic* VII, 517b-c.
35	Ibid.*Meno*, 86-96.
36	Ibid. *Republic* I, 353d2-354a2.
37	Ibid. *Gorgias*, 507b5-c.
38	Ibid, *Republic* VIII, 562b.
39	*Republic VII*, 526d1-e1.

40 Ibid. *Republic I*, 328c5-d3.
41 Ibid. *Republic I*, 330d4-7.
42 Ibid. *Republic I*, 334a3.
43 Ibid. *Republic I*, 334b5-6.
44 Ibid. *Republic I,* 334e8-10
45 Ibid. *Republic 1*, 335d11-12.
46 Ibid. *Republic I*, 334d10-13.
47 Ibid. *Republic I*, 335b2.
48 Ibid. *Republic I*, 336b3-5.
49 Ibid. *Republic I*, 336c4-d3.
50 Ibid. *Republic I*, 350c3-4.
51 Ibid. *Republic I*, 353a-e, 354c.
52 Ibid. See *Republic I*.
53 Ibid. See *Republic II*.
54 Ibid. *Republic II*, 358b2-5.
55 Ibid. *Republic II*, 359c9-360b.
56 Ibid. *Republic II*, 364c7-e2.
57 Ibid. *Republic II*, 362d-366d5.
58 Ibid. *Republic II*, 369a4-5.
59 Ibid. *Republic V*, 473c10-e2.
60 Ibid. *Republic III*, 415a1-5.
61 Ibid. *Republic IV*, 427e4-7.
62 Ibid. *Republic IV*, 441c3-5.
63 Ibid. *Republic IV*, 440e-444e.
64 Ibid. *Republic V*, 476b7-8.
65 Ibid. See *Republic VI*.
66 Ibid. *Republic VI, See the Analogy of the Divided Line.*

67	Ibid. *Republic VII*, 517b-c4. *See the Allegory of the Cave.*
68	Ibid. *Phaedo*, 100a-e.
69	Ibid. *Republic VII*, 517b7-c4.
70	Ibid. *Republic VII*, 521d13-e1.
71	Ibid. *Republic VII*, 522c4-6.
72	Ibid. *Republic VII*, 526c.
73	Ibid. *Republic VII*, 528b.
74	Ibid. *Republic VII*, 528d-e.
75	Ibid. *Republic VII*, 530d.
76	Ibid. *Republic VII*, 533d3-4.
77	Ibid. *Republic X*, 614b-618c.
78	Ibid. *Republic X*, 621c2-4.
79	Ibid. Apology 32c3-e2.
80	Ibid. *Apology*, 18e3-19a1-2.
81	Ibid. *Apology*, 35d10-11.
82	Ibid. *Apology*, 41d1-2.
83	Ibid. Cratylus, 400c. Hermogenes was with Socrates on the day of his death.
84	Irwin Terence, *Plato's Ethics*, New York and Oxford, Oxford University Press, 1995, p. 296.
85	Augustine of Hippo, *The City of God*, trans. Henry Bettenson, Harmondsworth, England, Penguin Classics, 1995.
86	Hendricks, Howard G. *Living by the Book: The Art and Science of Reading the Bible,* Chicago, Moody Publishers, 2007
87	Conner, Kevin J., *Tabernacle of Moses*, Portland, Oregon, City Christian Publishing, p. 17. The credit goes to this book for the descriptions of the construction and furnishings of the Tabernacle of

Moses that this author has rephrased in her own words after studying the Biblical descriptions.

88	Plato, *Plato: Complete Works, Symposium*, 174a6-9.
89	Ibid. *Symposium*, 179b4-5.
90	Ibid. *Symposium*, 198b1-3.
91	Ibid. *Symposium*, 199d2-3.
92	Ibid. *Symposium*, 204a1-6.
93	Ibid. *Symposium*, 204b3-6.
94	Ibid. *Symposium*, 211e2-212a1.
95	Ibid. *Symposium*, 211c-d
96	Ibid. *Alcibiades*, 131c.

www.ingramcontent.com/pod-product-compliance
Lightning Source LLC
Chambersburg PA
CBHW051646040426
42446CB00009B/1006